Milan Fashion Campus

SENSUAL FASHION ILLUSTRATION

Milan Fashion Campus®
WWW.MILANFASHIONCAMPUS.EU

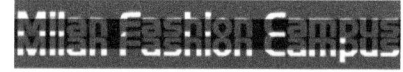

SENSUAL FASHION ILLUSTRATION

This book will show you how a simple image could be transformed into a fashion illustration design.

The template is a design made by hand, taking inspiration from a picture.

The design has to be very neat and simple with just main shape.

After scanning the template, we're ready to work it out in photoshop, there are many techniques that we're going to use. At the beginning, to get a concept of the style we could use for example: greyish tones, colorfull, pastel colors etc...

The kind of background whether as a real photo or as a sketch.
Our goal is to achieve the harmony of the design and colors making clear what it's represented.

There are illustrations made for designers of accessories, such as shoes and jewelry, to emphasize the product for a campaign or a magazine cover page, but also illustrations of poses or the most important outfit from runway collections.

Here we are, now enjoy to create your amazing fashion illustration!

INTRODUCTION:

A new and different way of thinking about fashion illustrations.
Images in this book include not only lines, edges and design techniques; what we want to represent is passion, sensuality and femininity.

Accessories, jewelry and poses are used to emphasize each female curve making all illustrations beautiful and attractive.
Our goal is to give you several options to express the feminine sensuality. You will find some soft illustrations, delicate and sweet with a touch of romance, while on the other side there are more explicit drawings with provocative poses and strong shades.
Broaden your point of view and exceed, don't think about imposed limits and discover how to combine fashion, art and illustration technique.

This book aims to be a tribute to women, especially to their ability to be fascinating.

Sensual Fashion Illustration Book: concept by Angelo Russica designs by Lorenzo Curti

BY Milan Fashion Campus - WWW.MILANFASHIONCAMPUS.EU

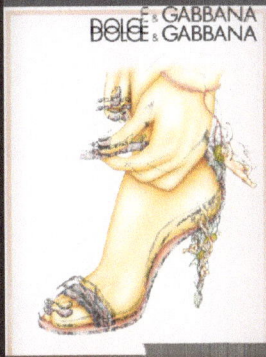
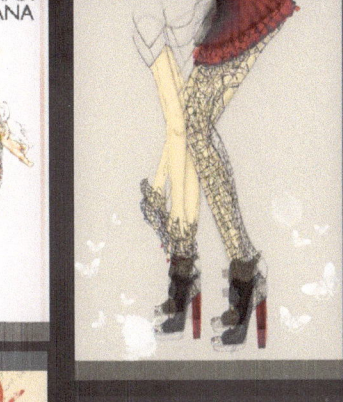
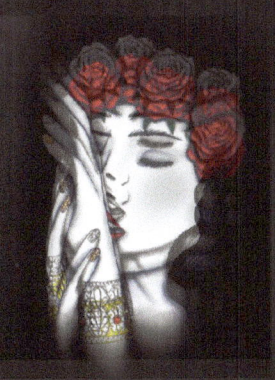
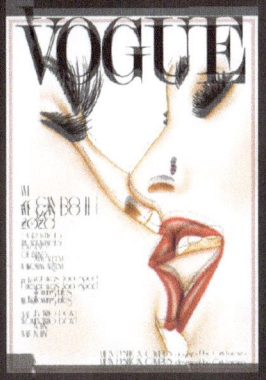
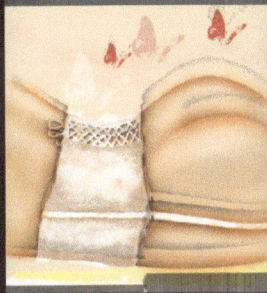
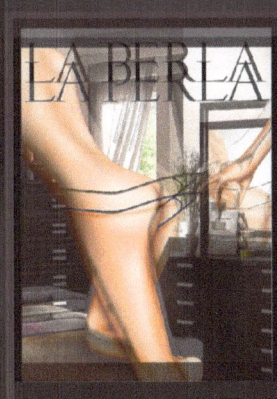
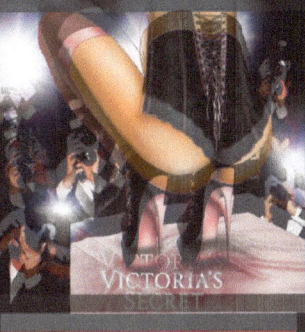
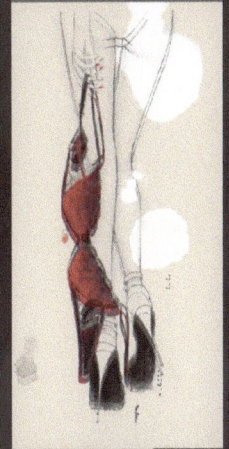
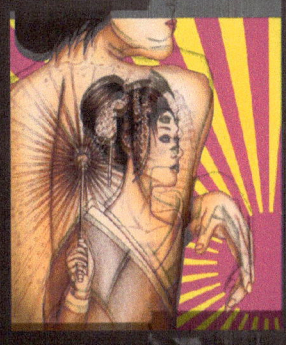
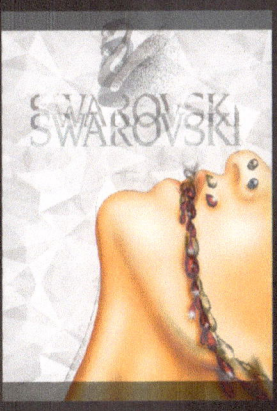
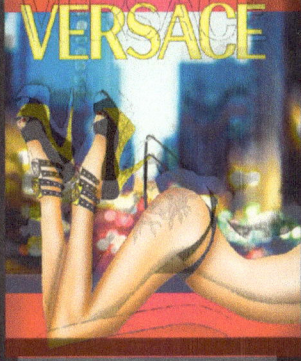
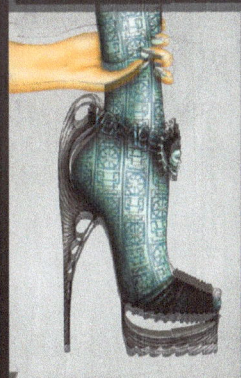
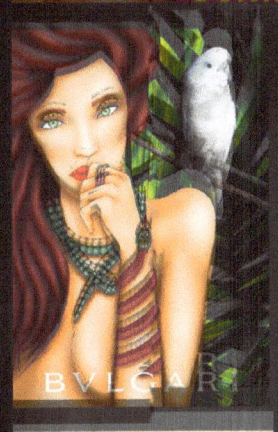
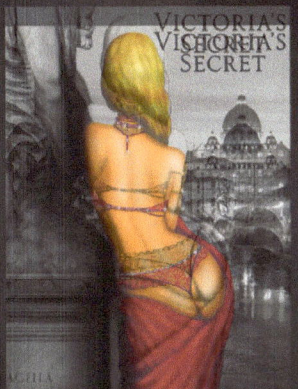
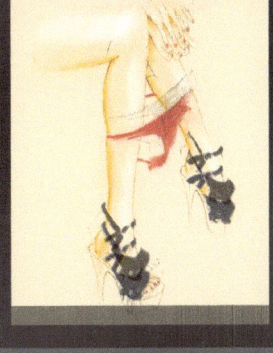
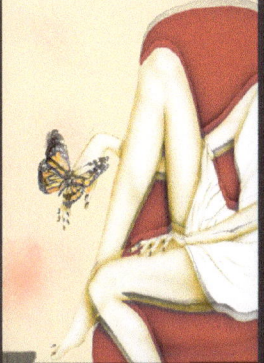
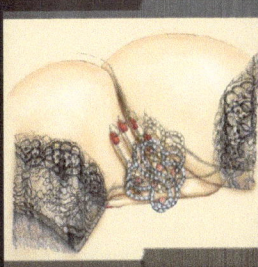

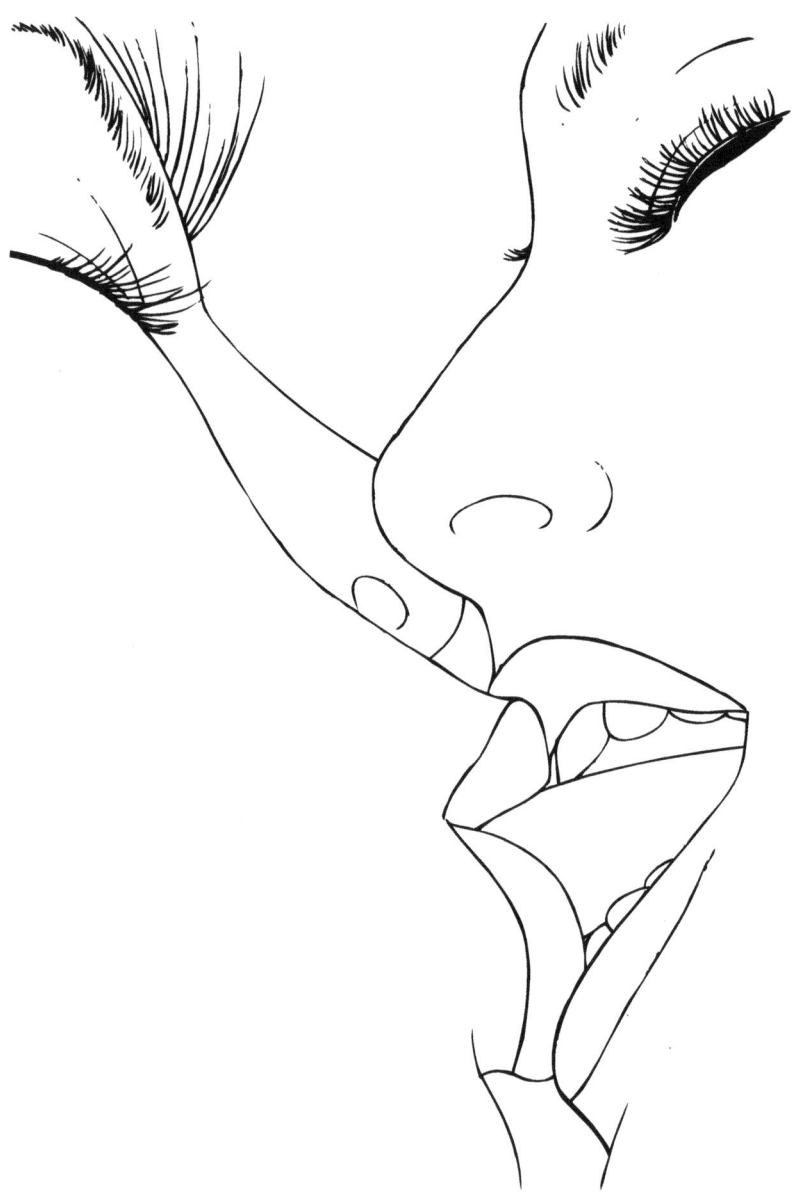

Milan Fashion Campus

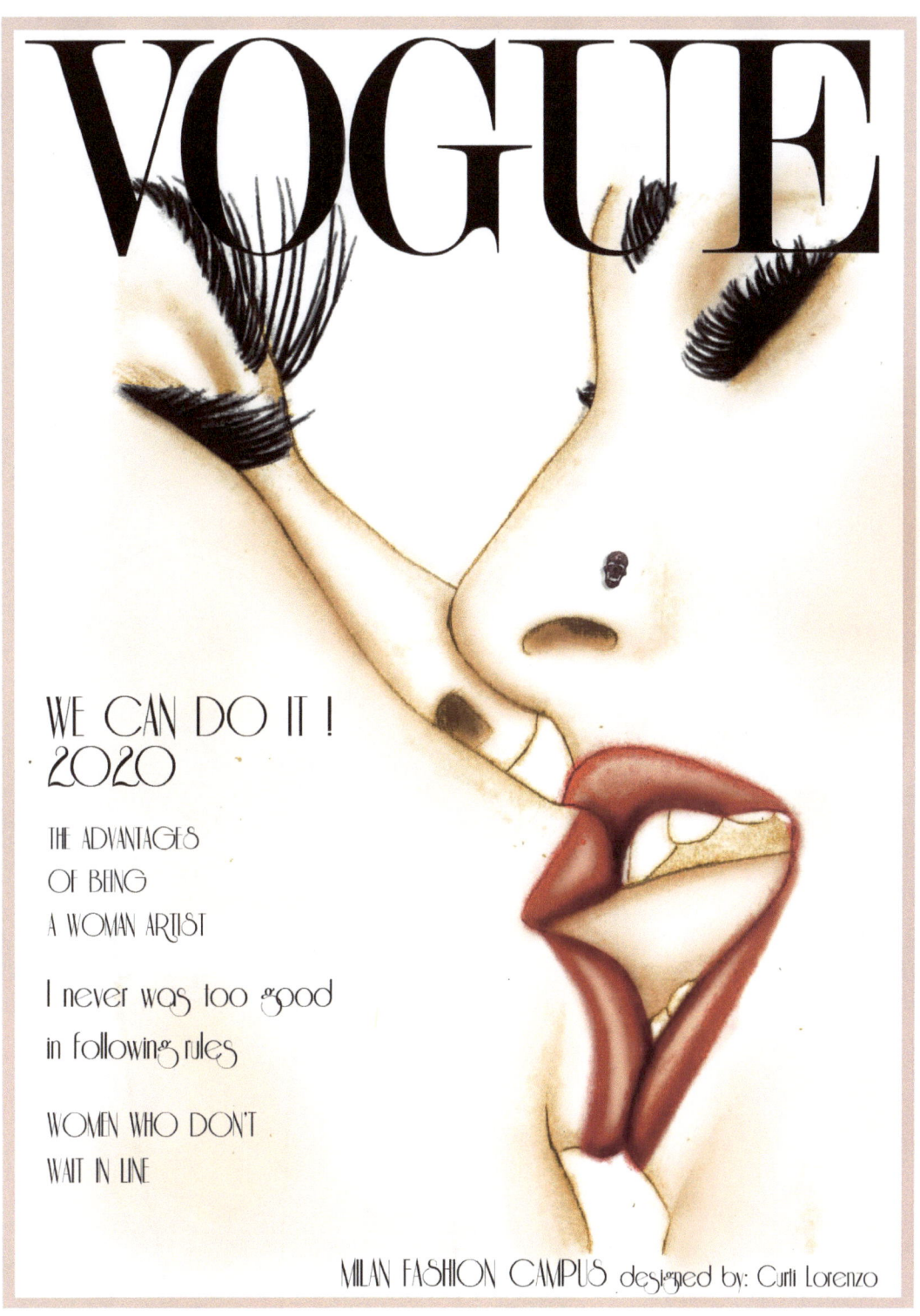

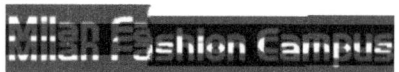

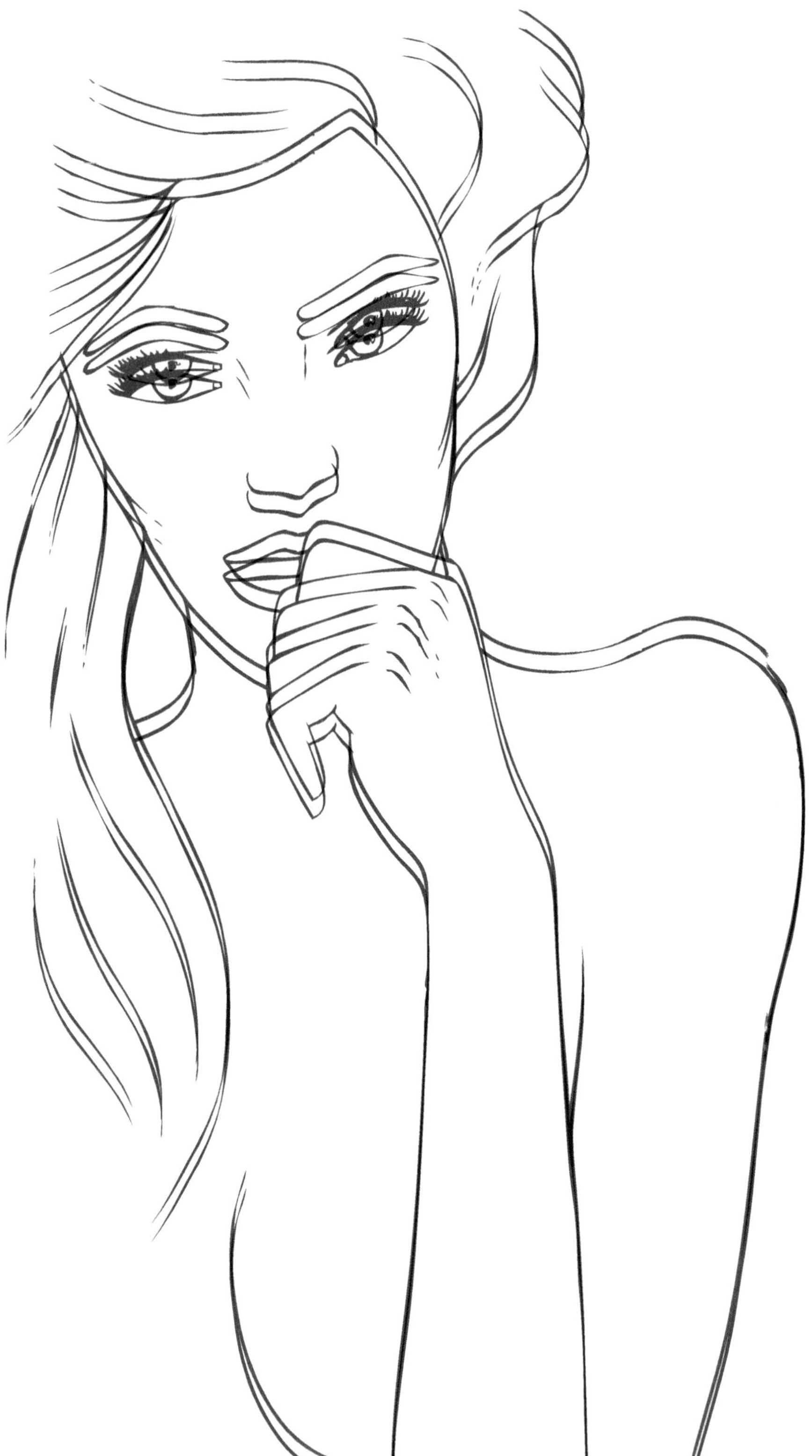

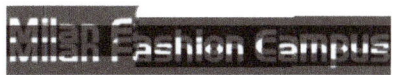

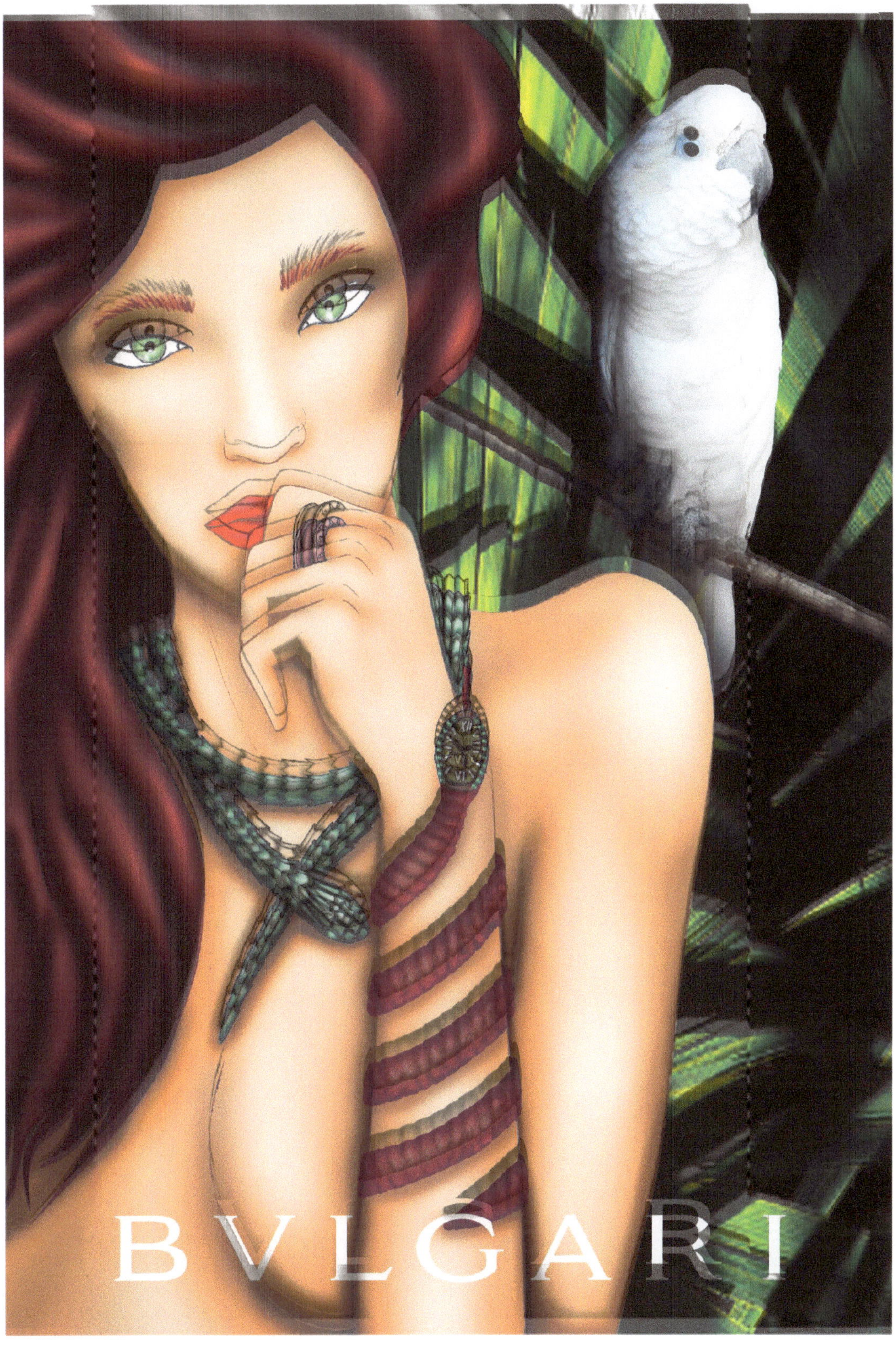

Milan Fashion Campus

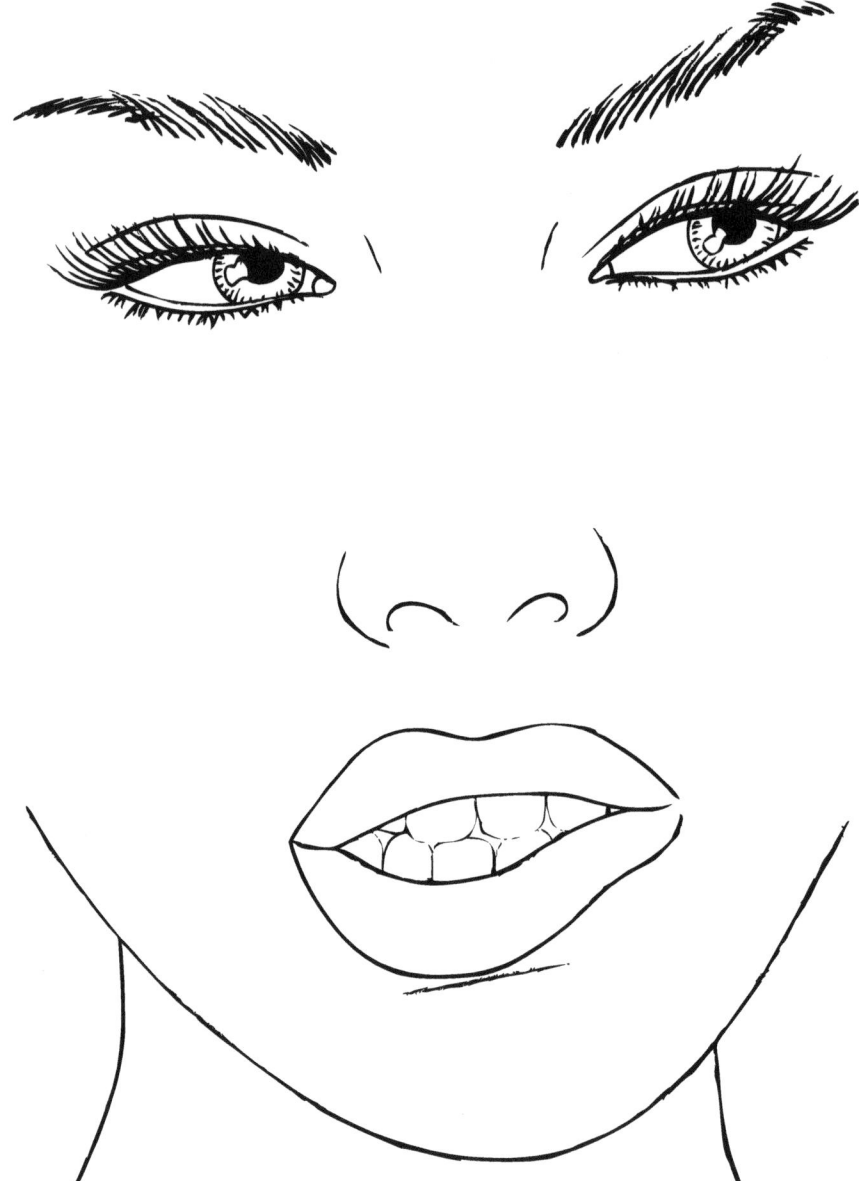

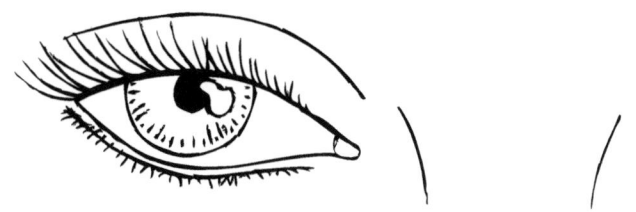
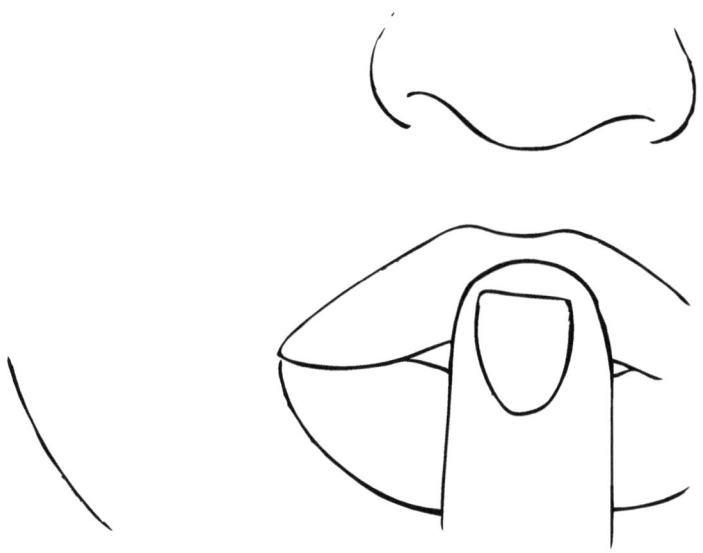

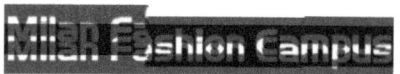

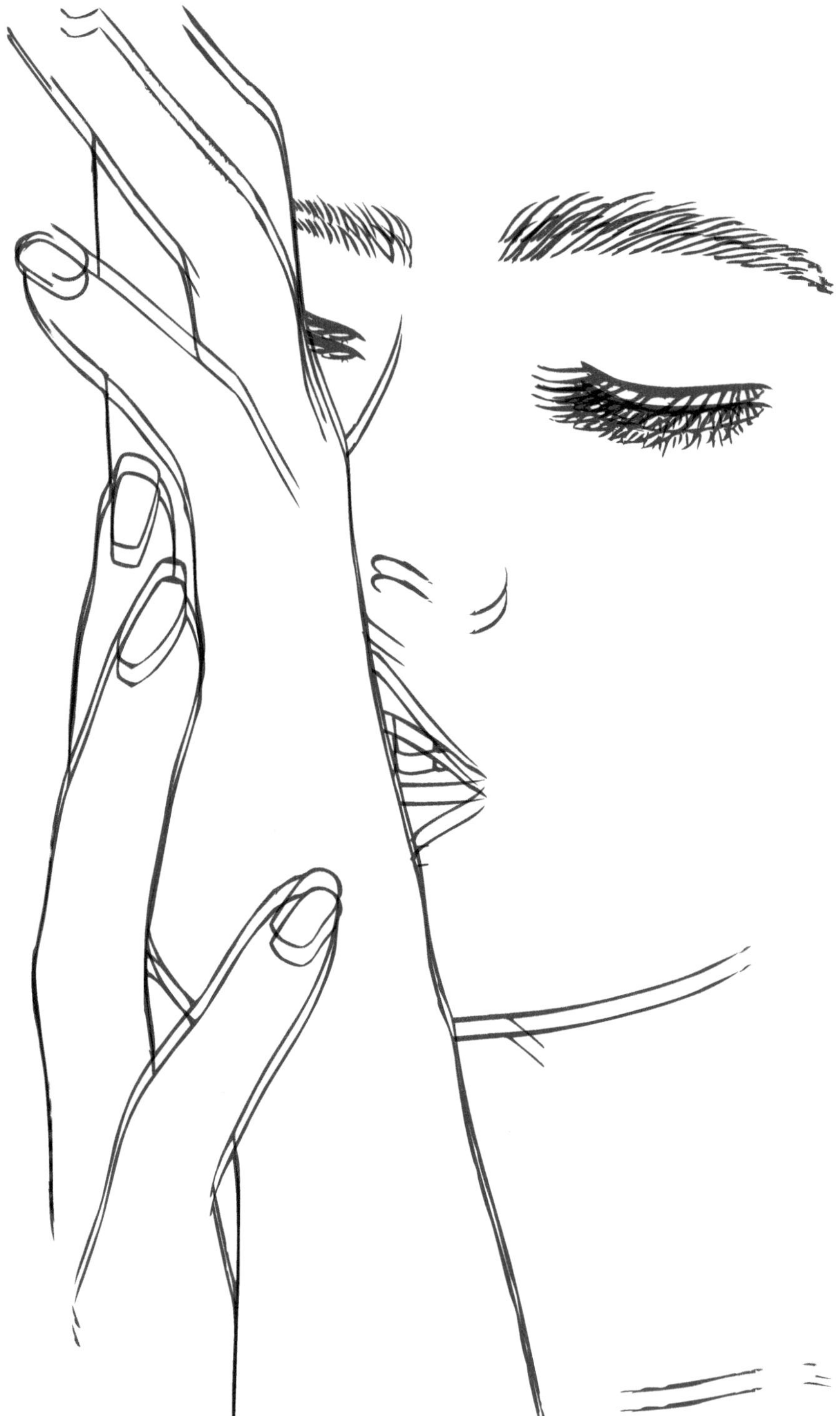

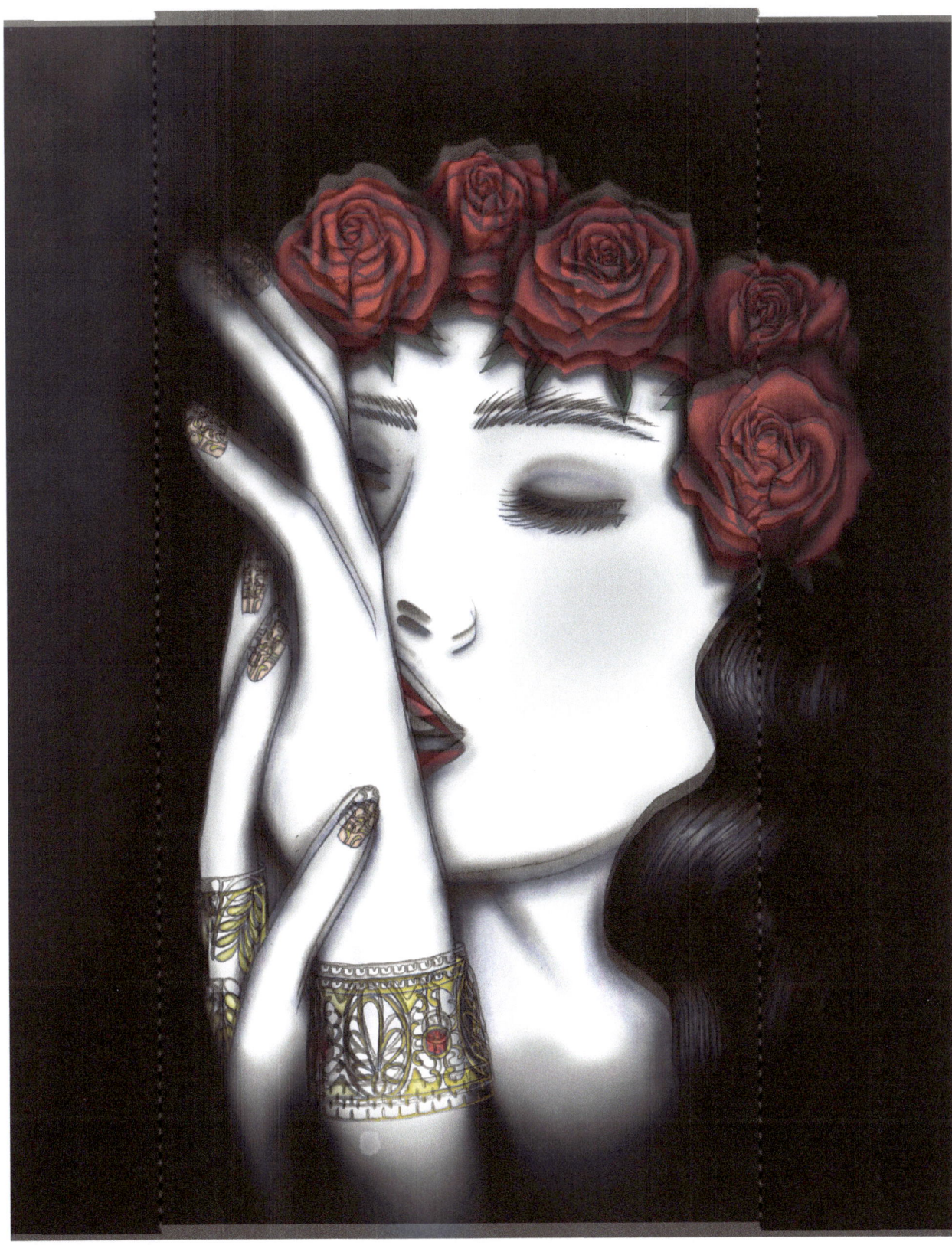

Milan Fashion Campus

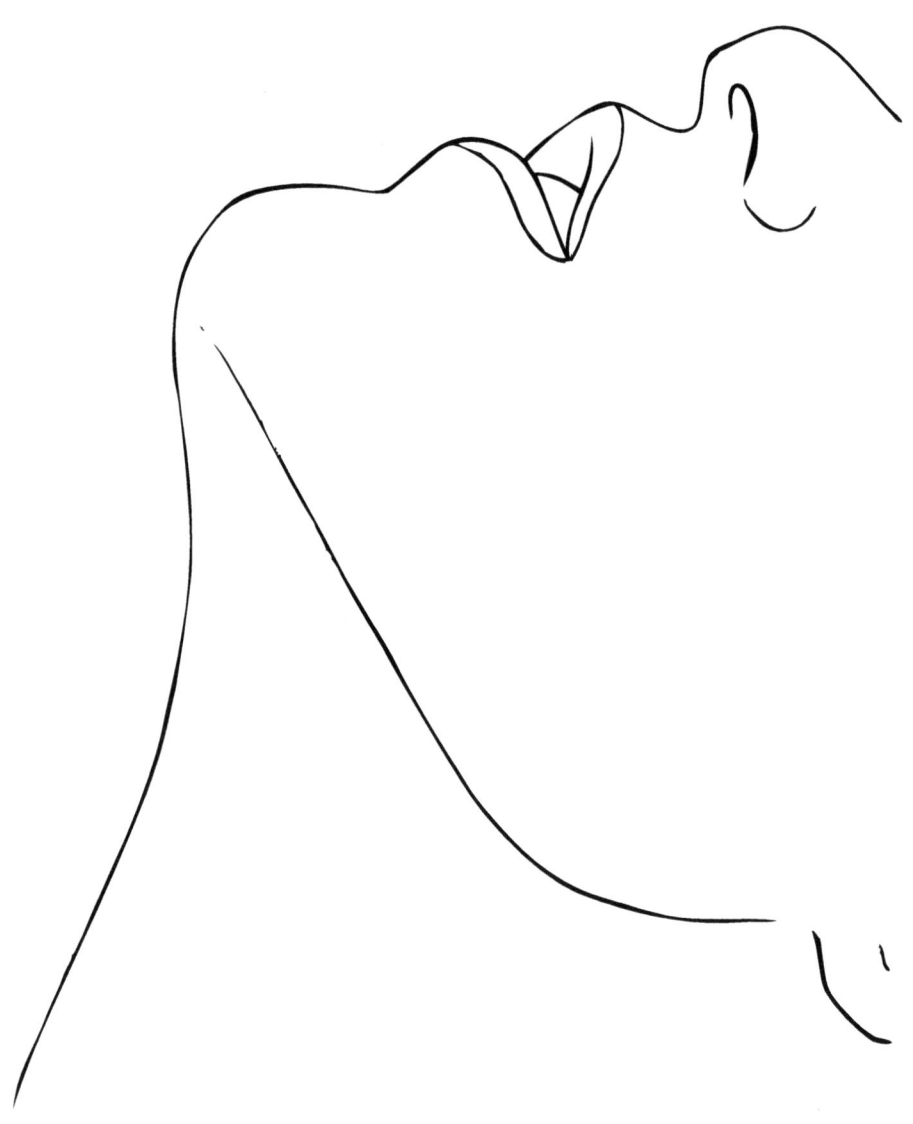

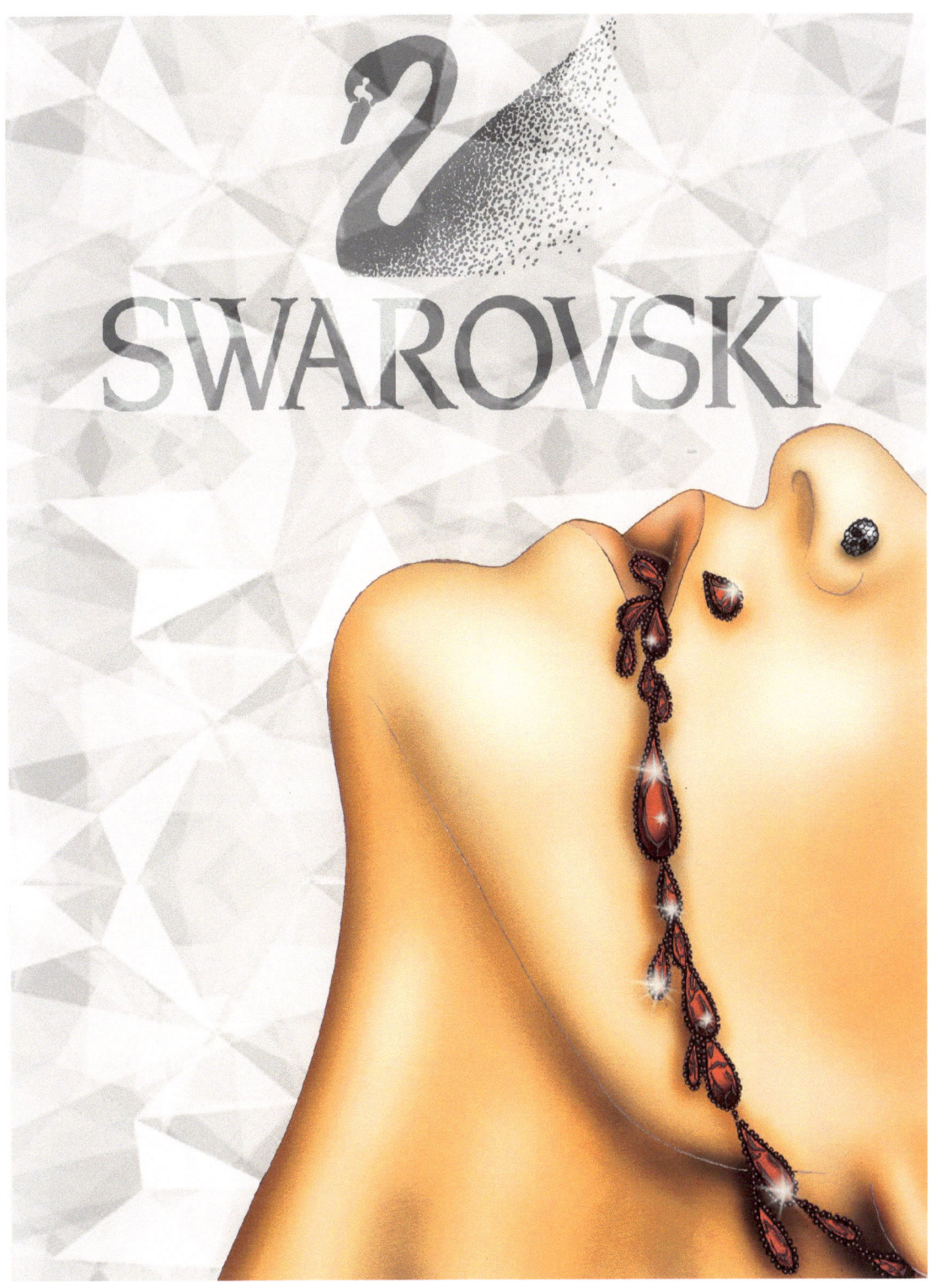

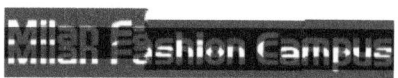

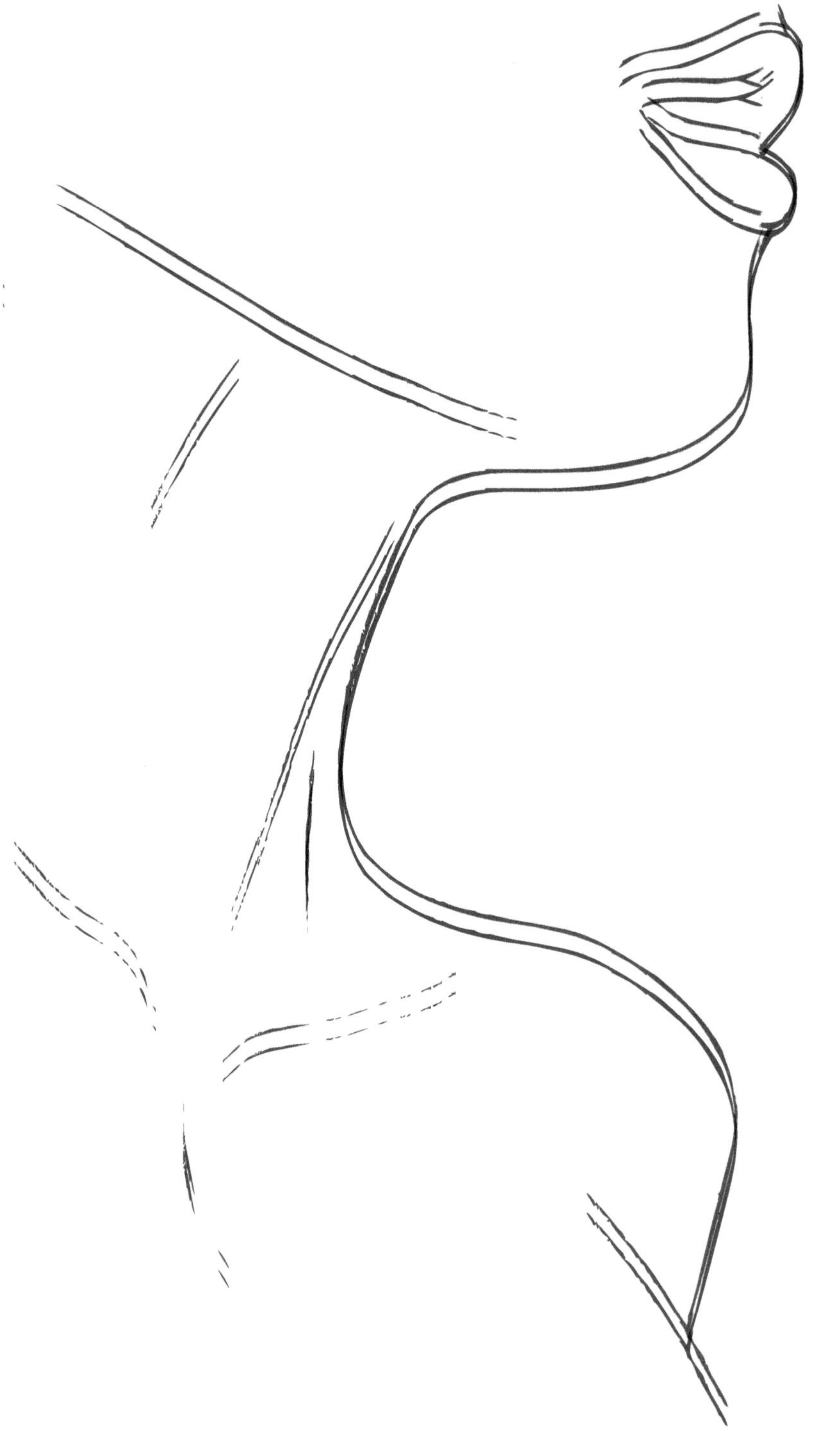

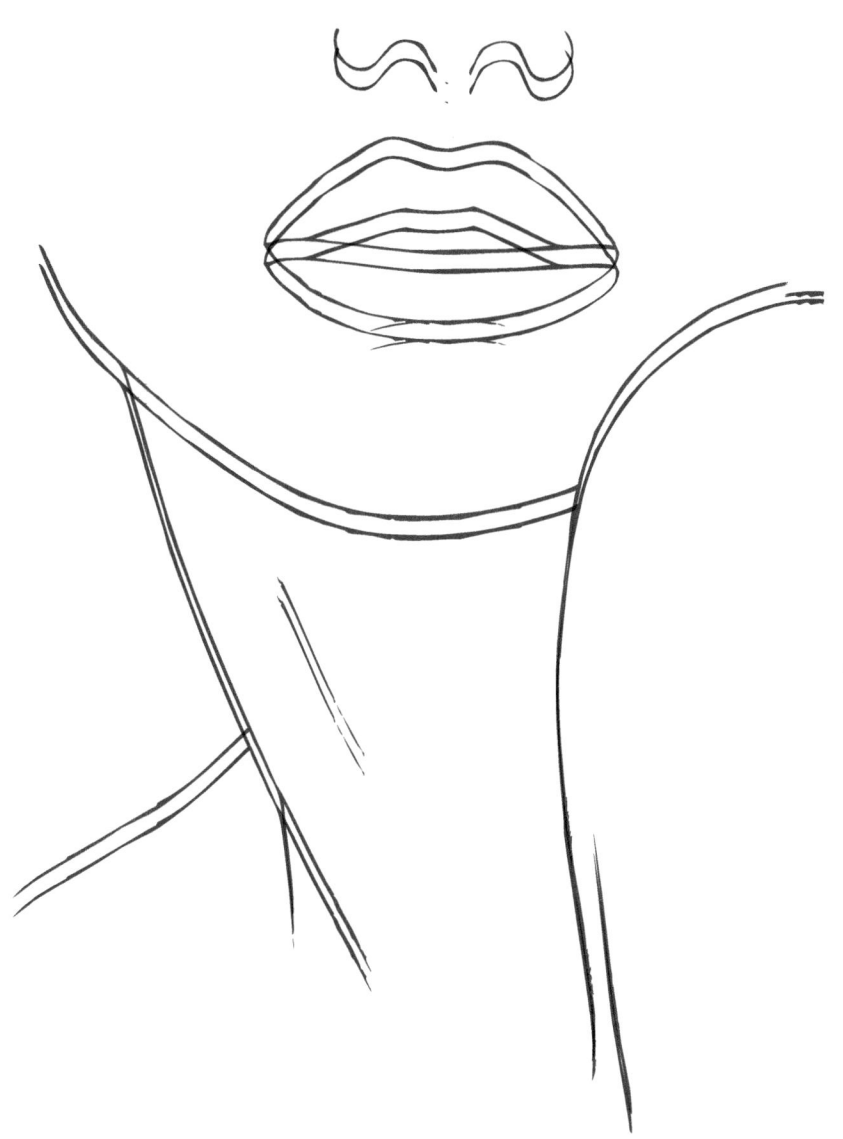

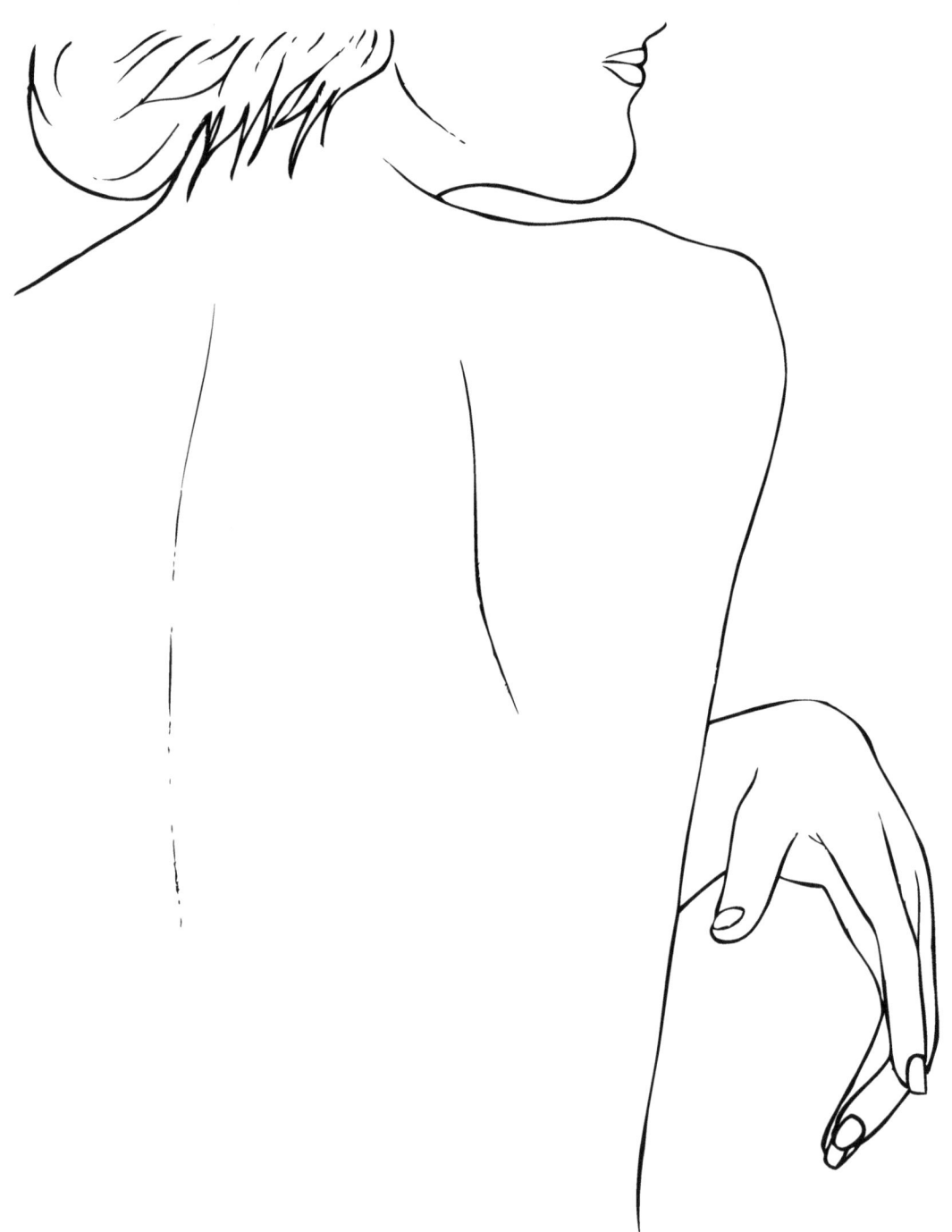

Milan Fashion Campus

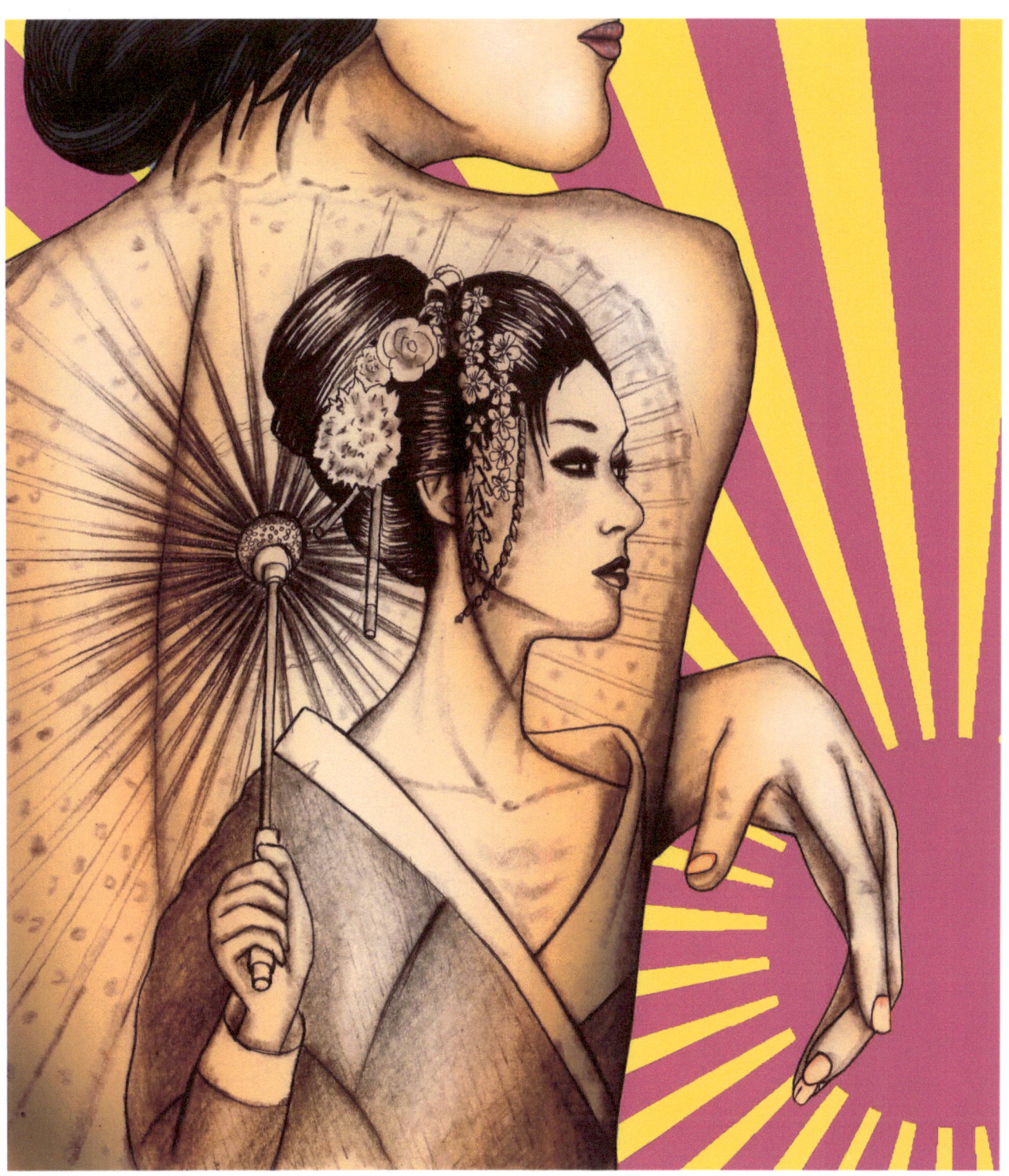

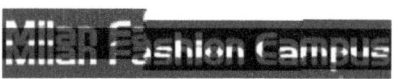

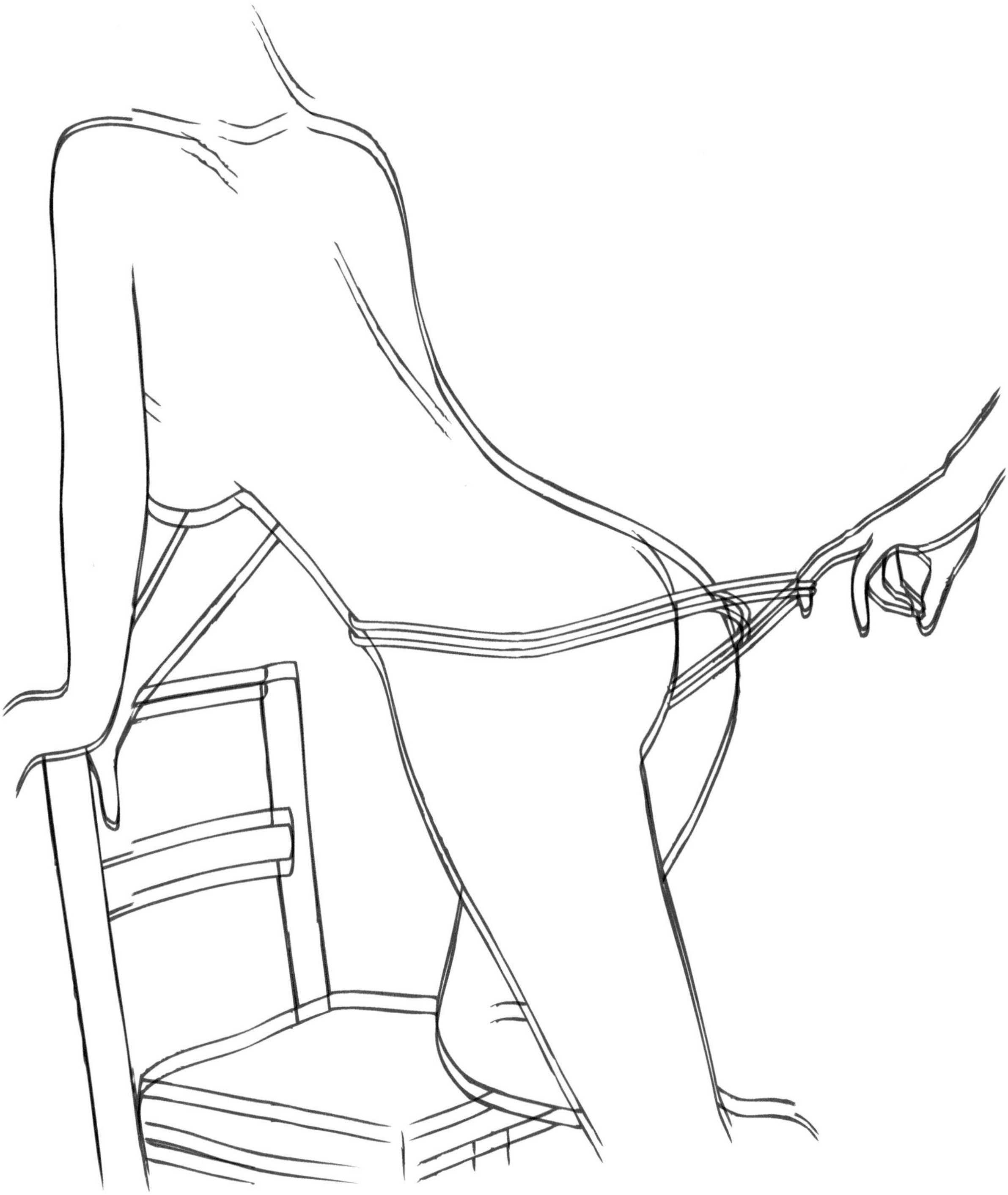

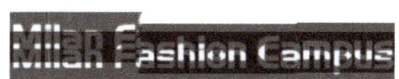

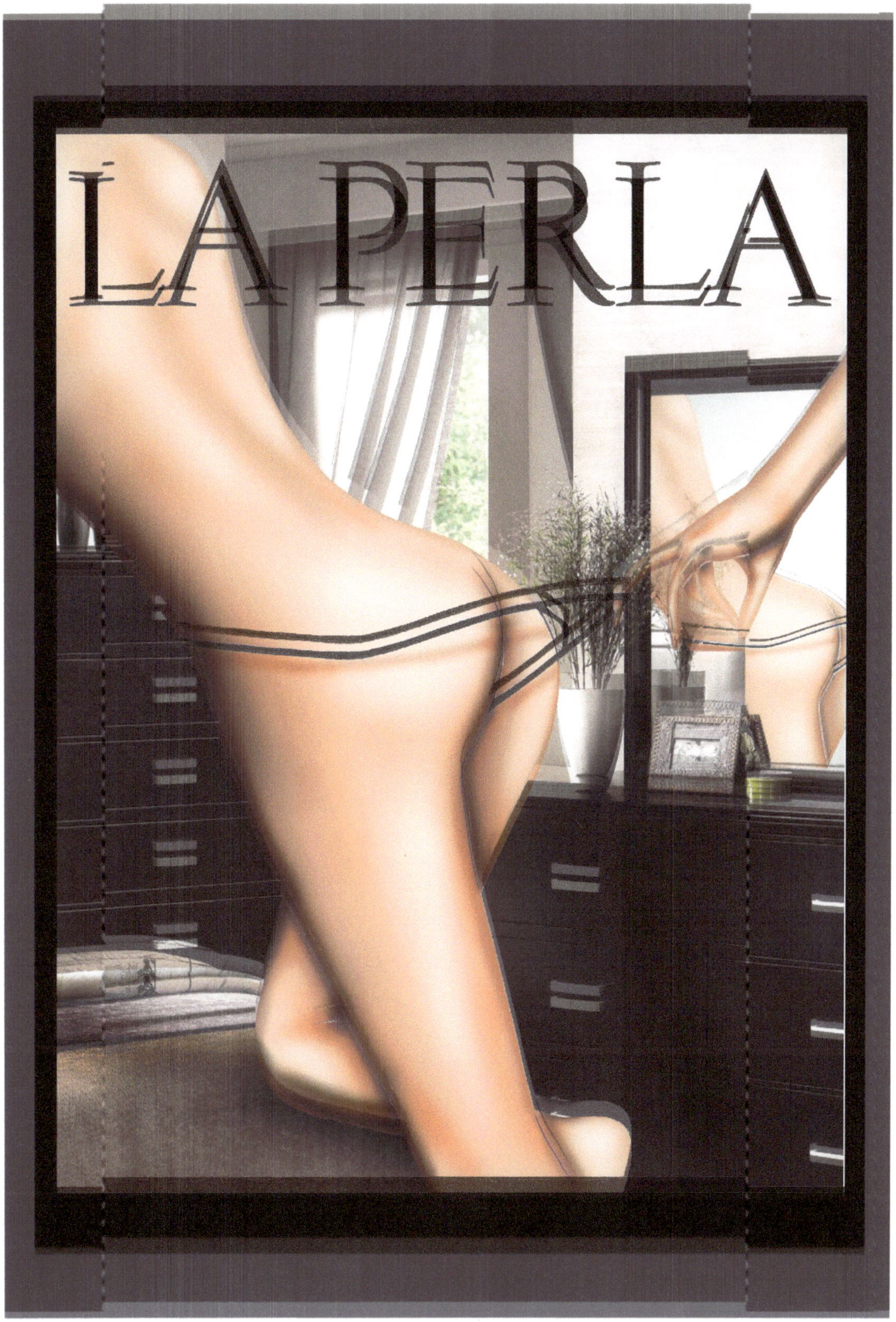

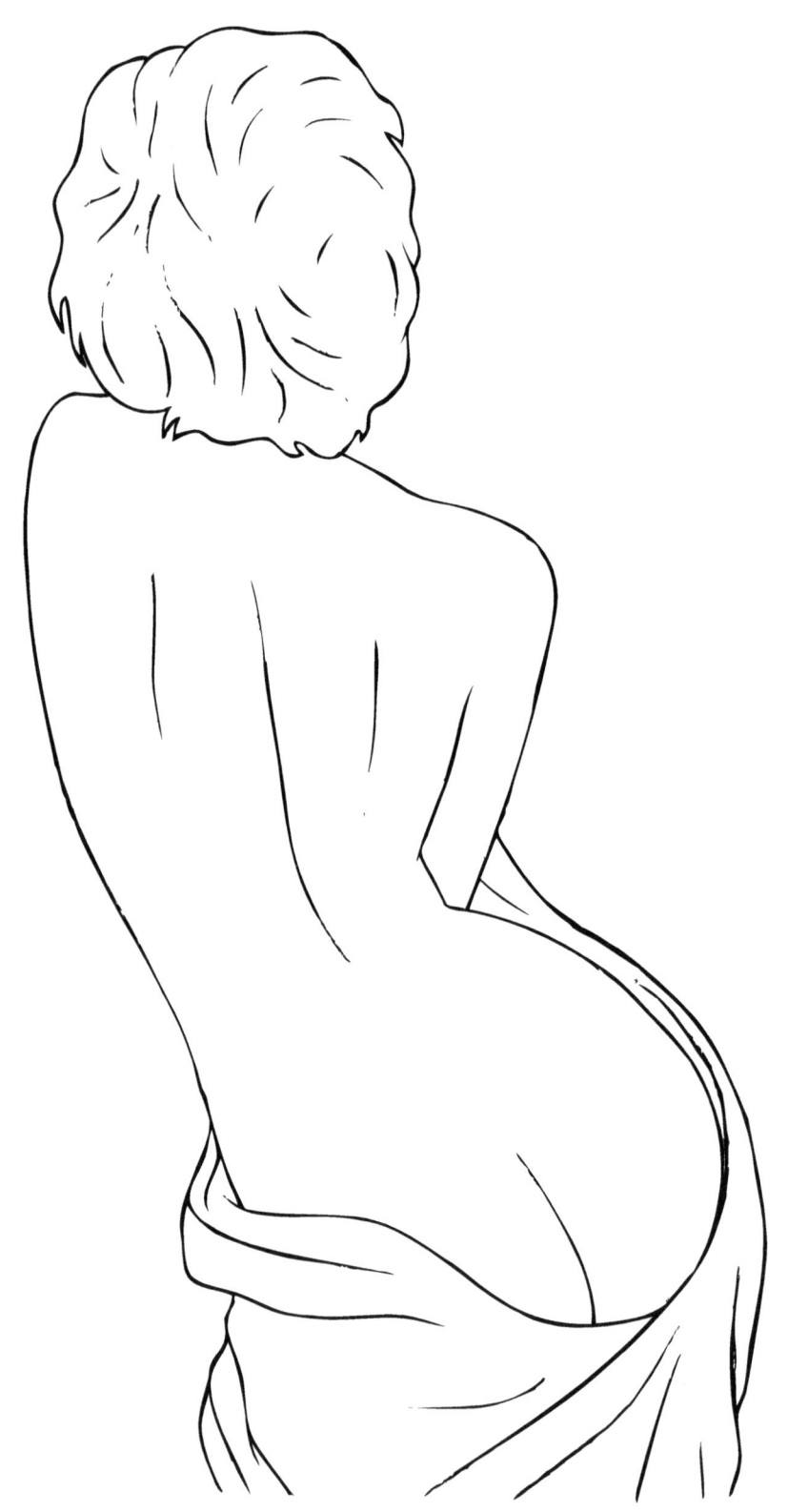

Milan Fashion Campus

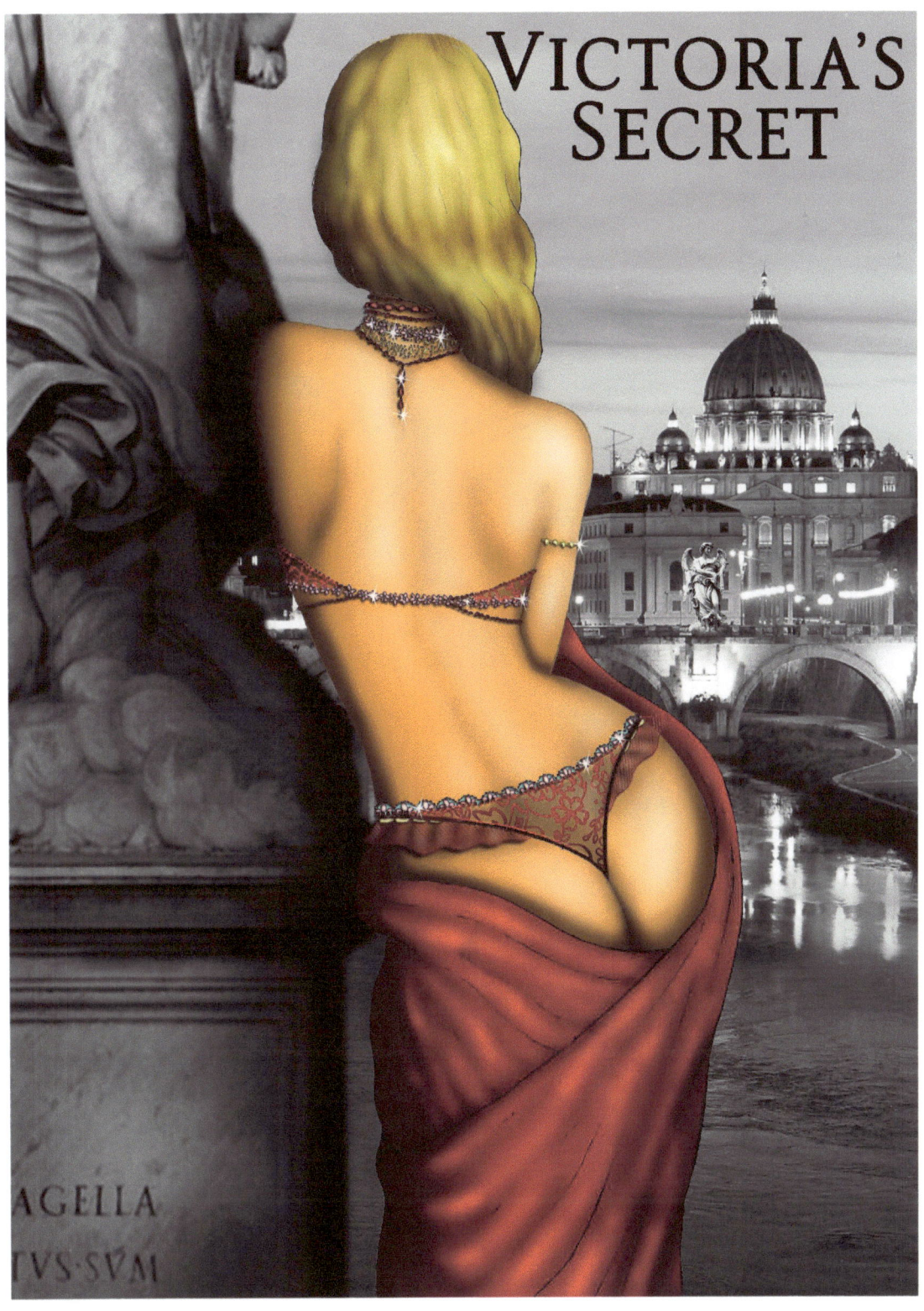

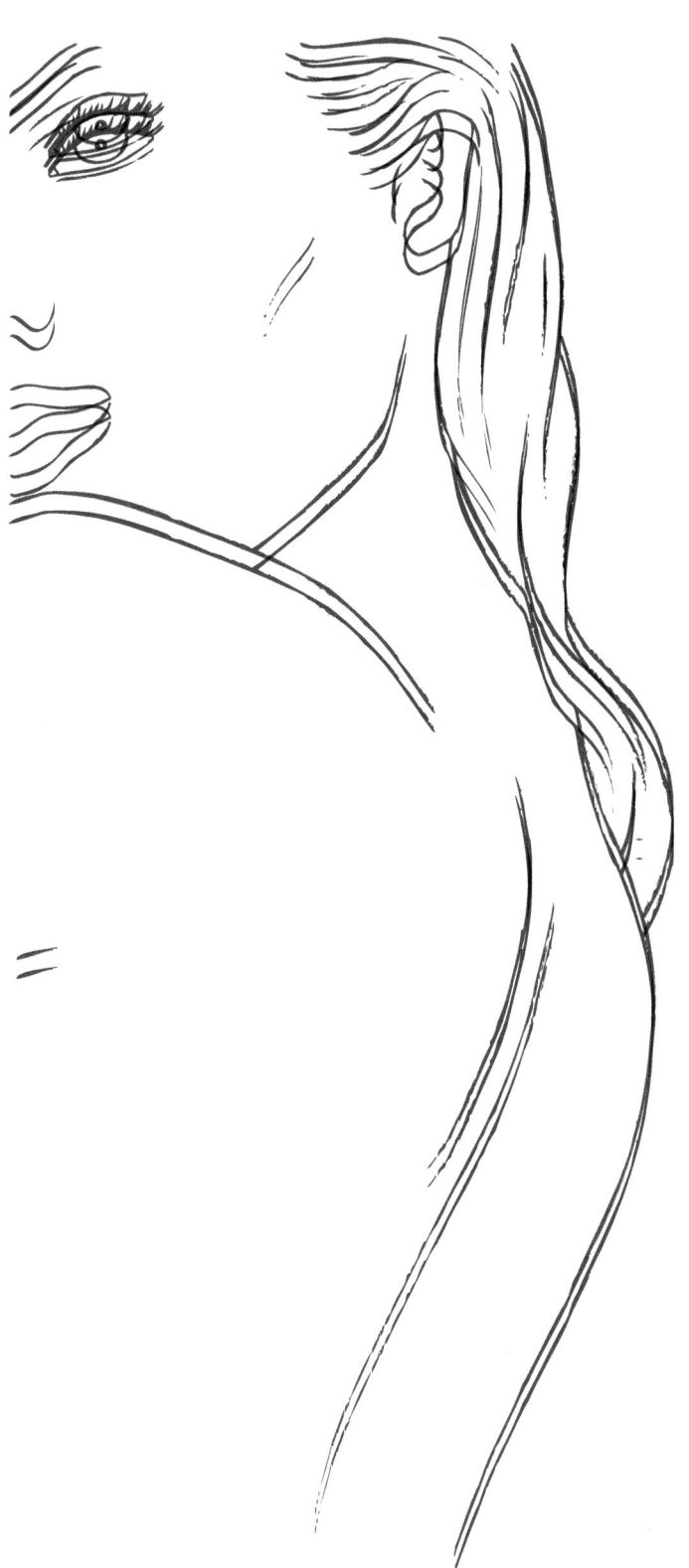

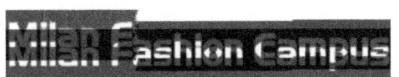
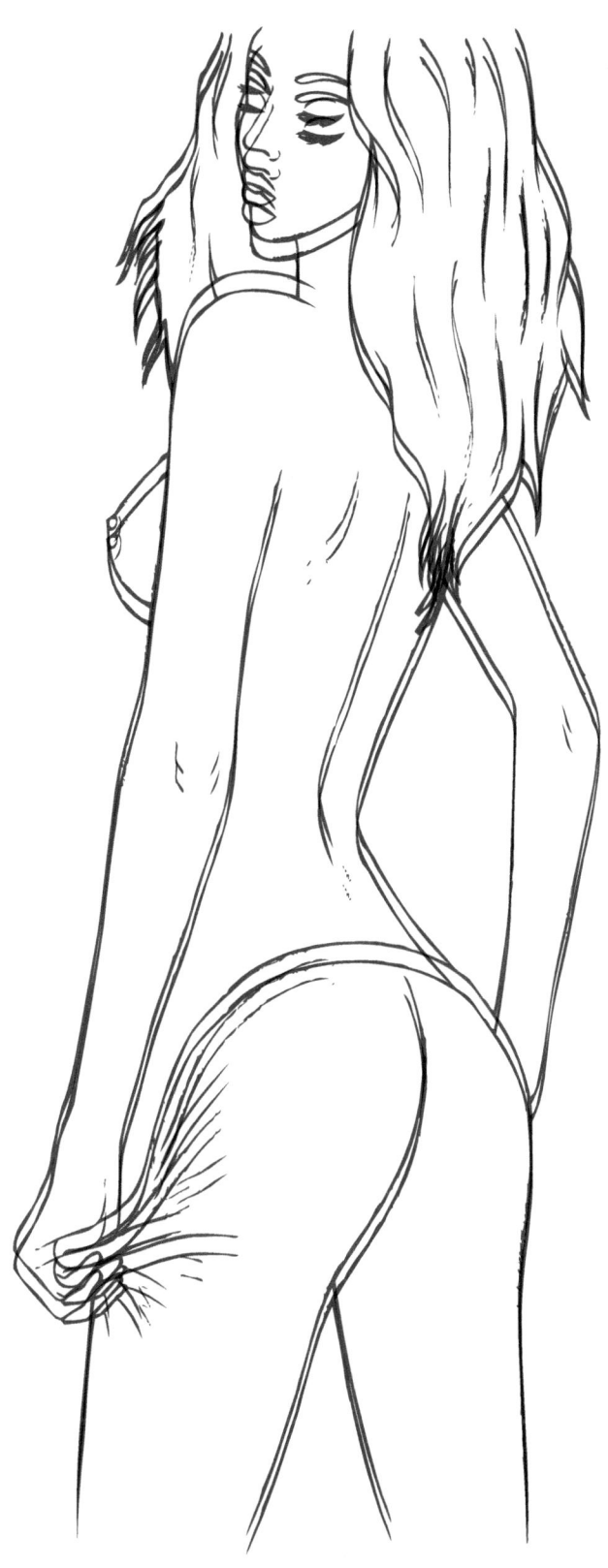

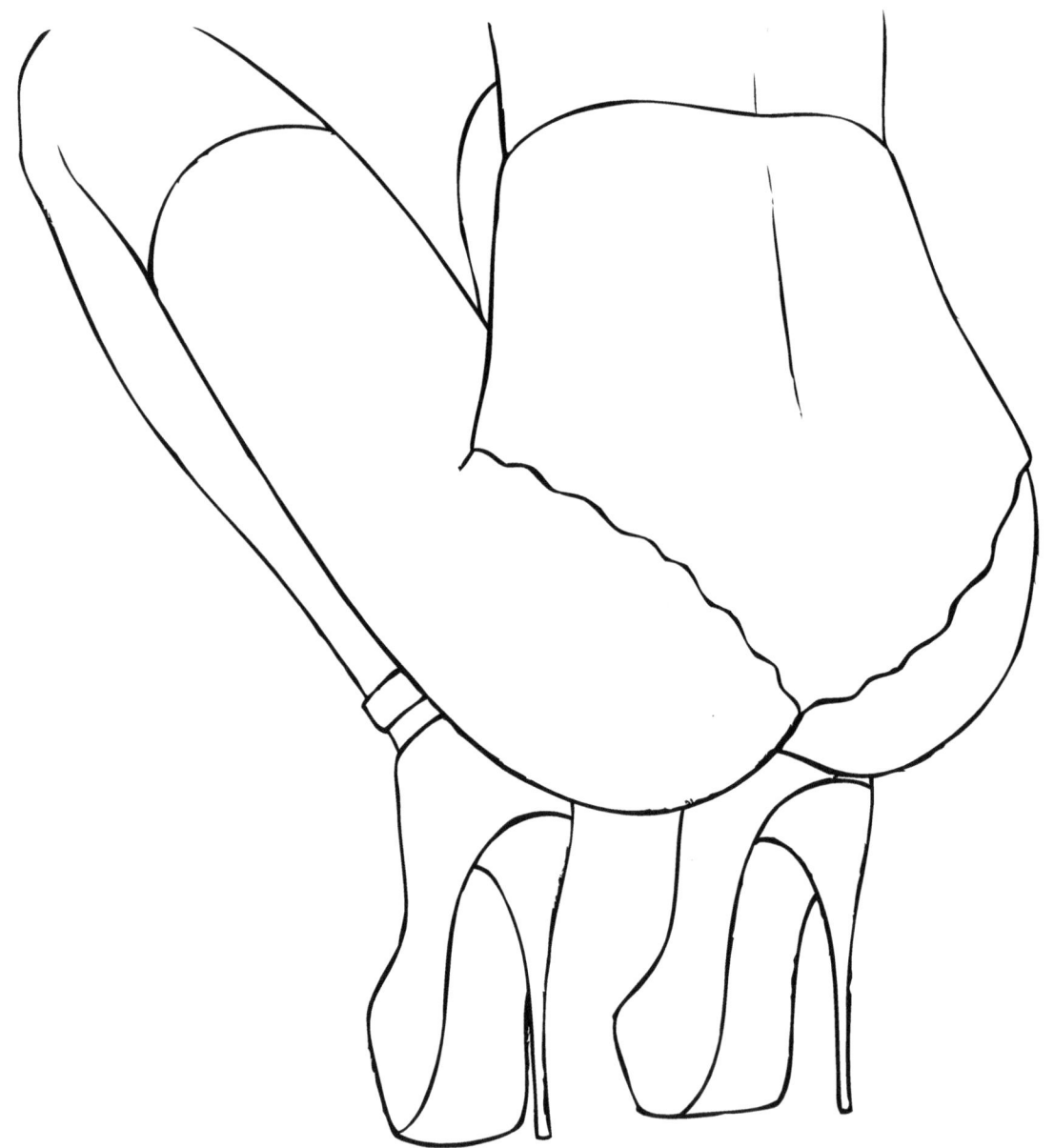

Milan Fashion Campus

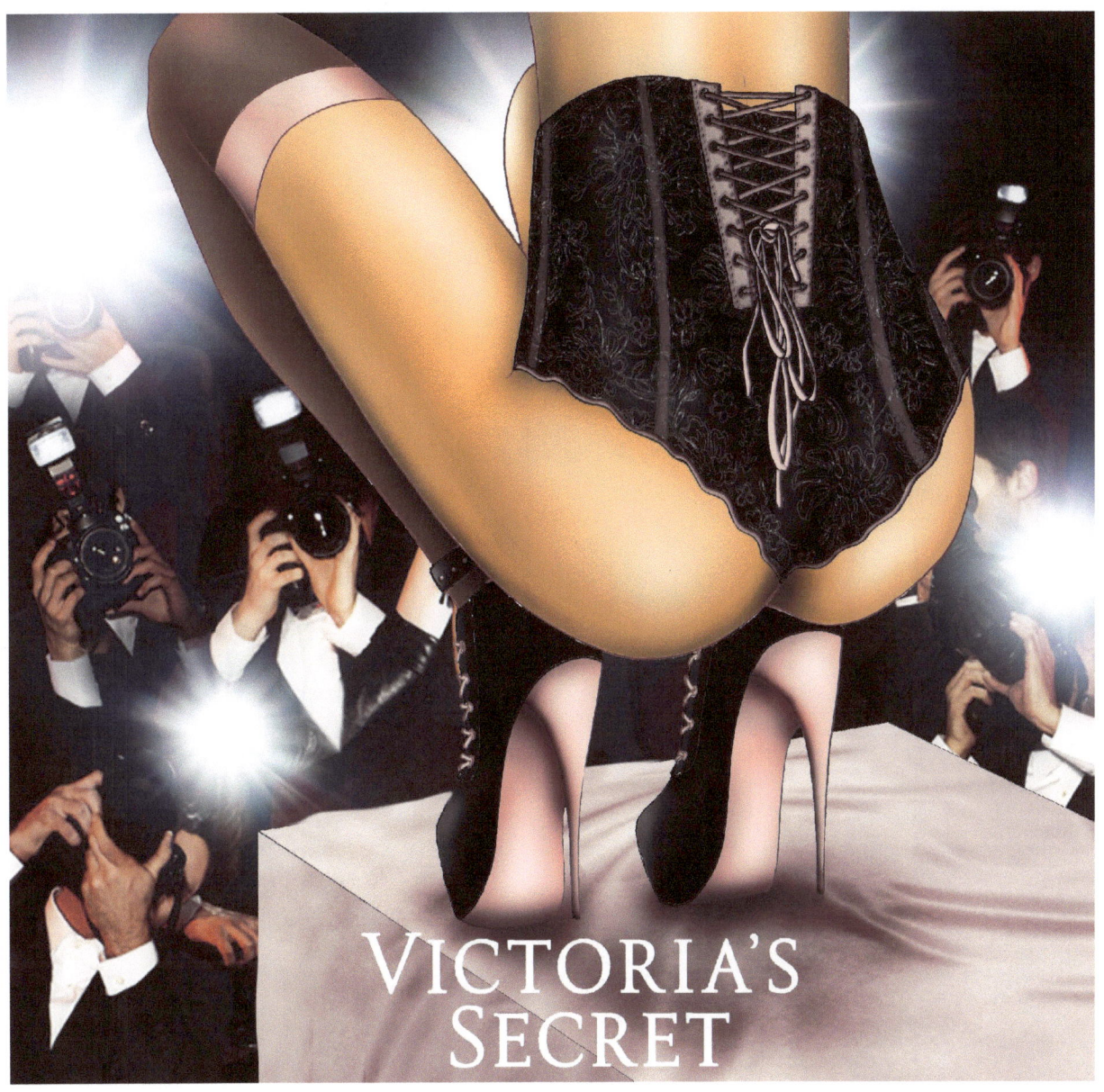

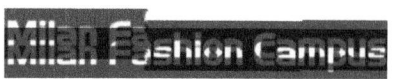

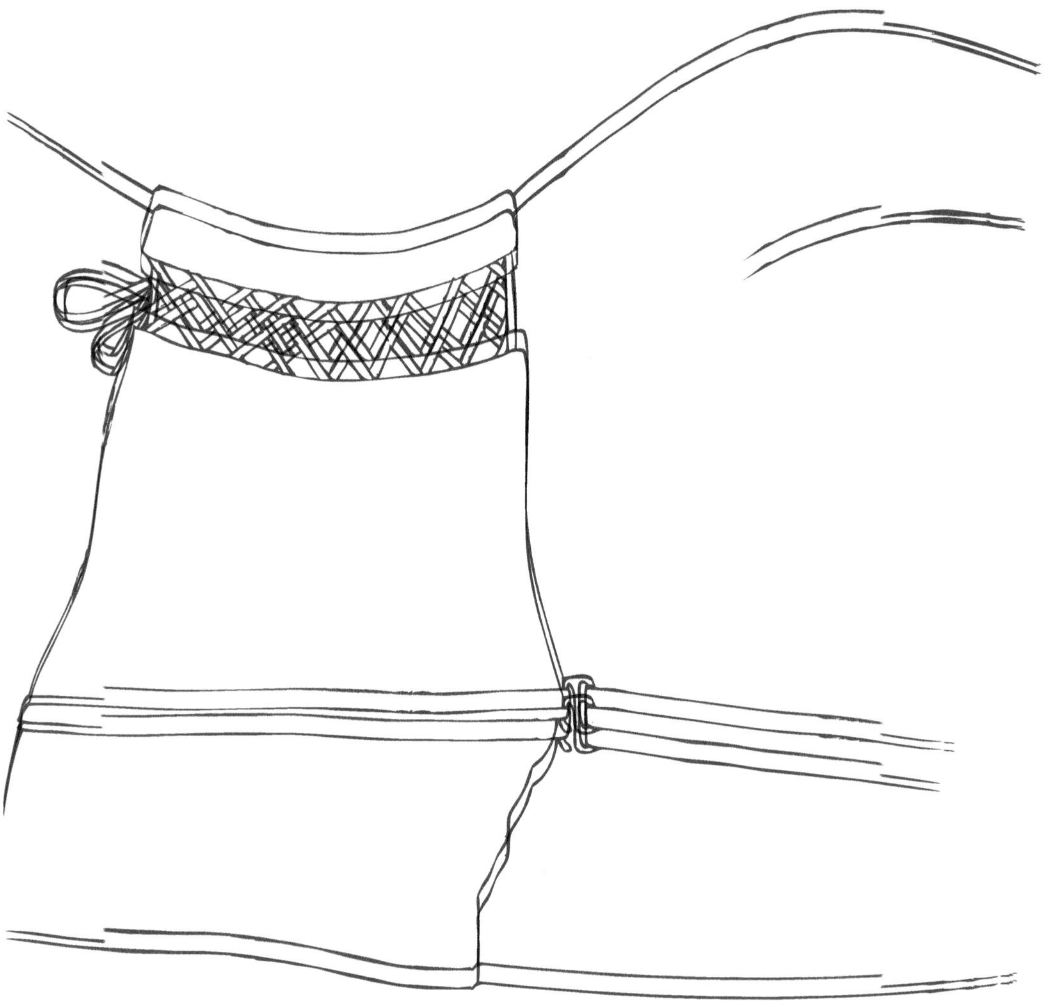

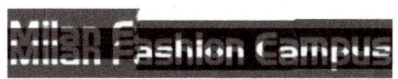

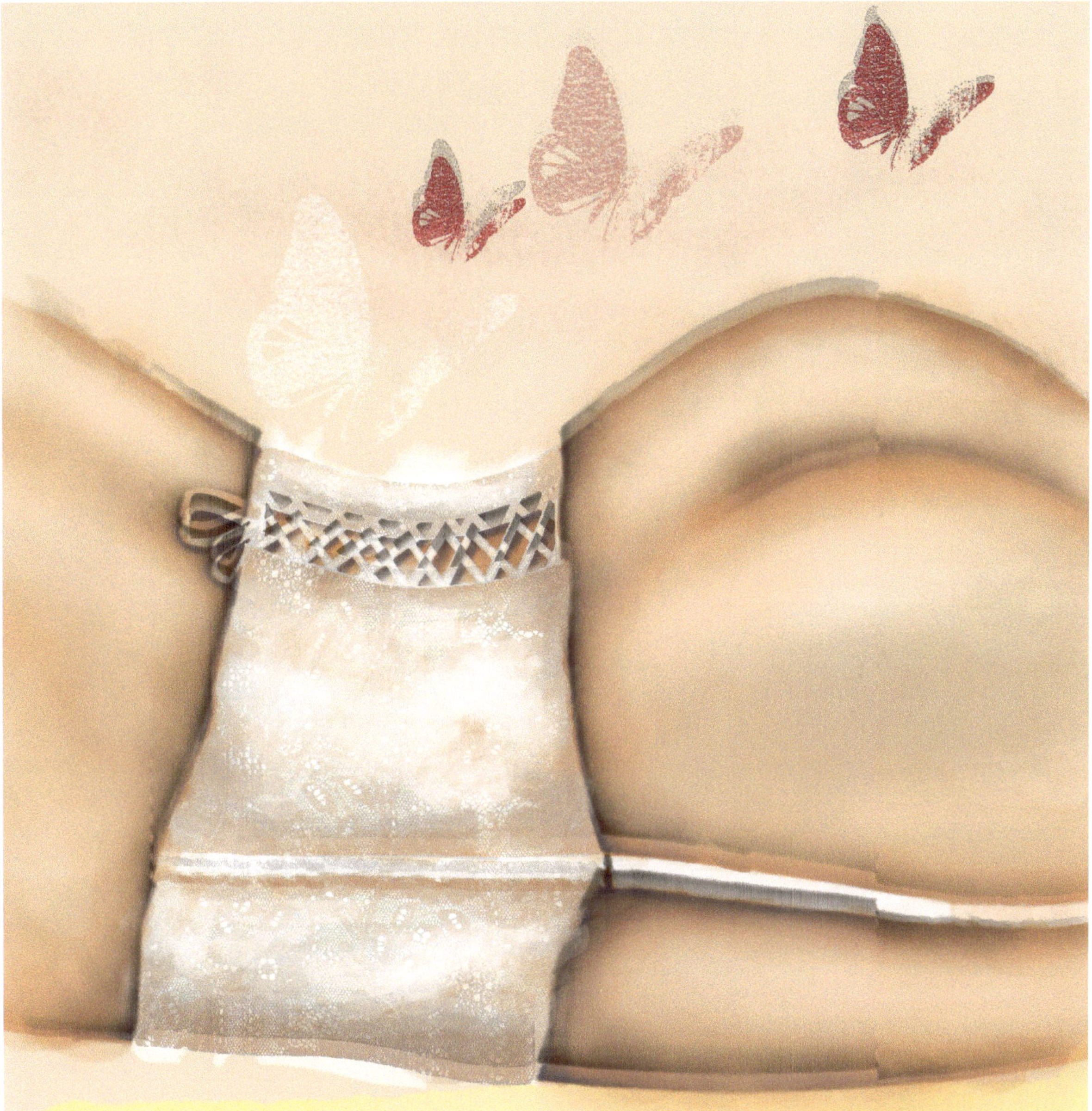

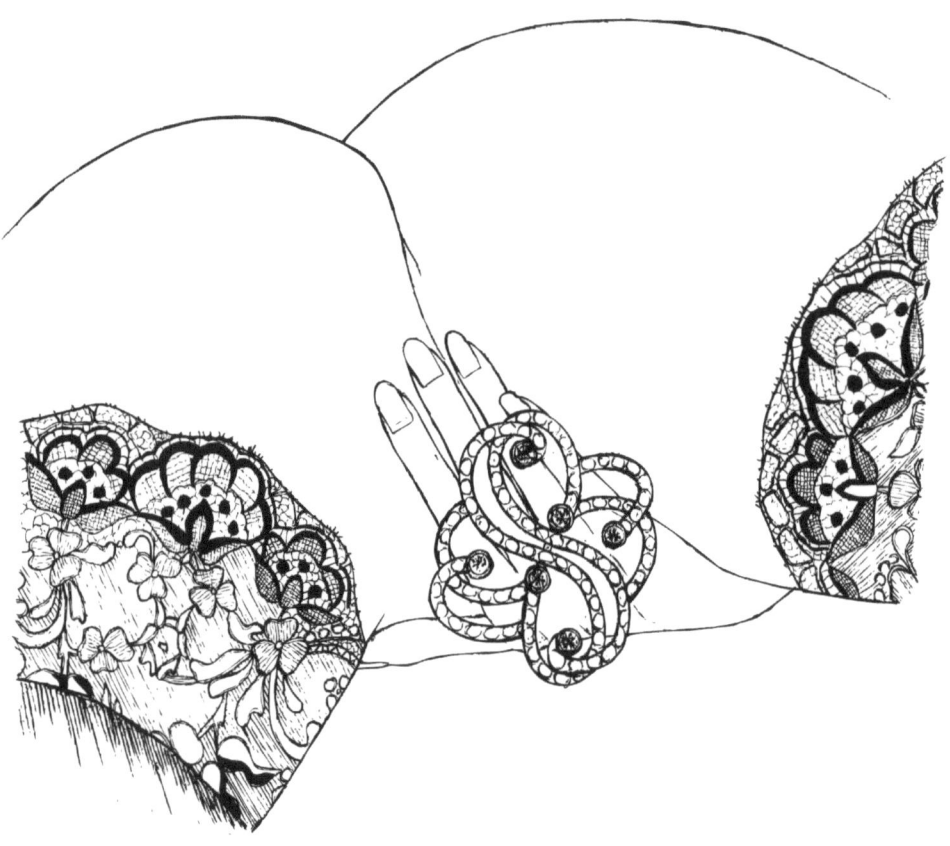

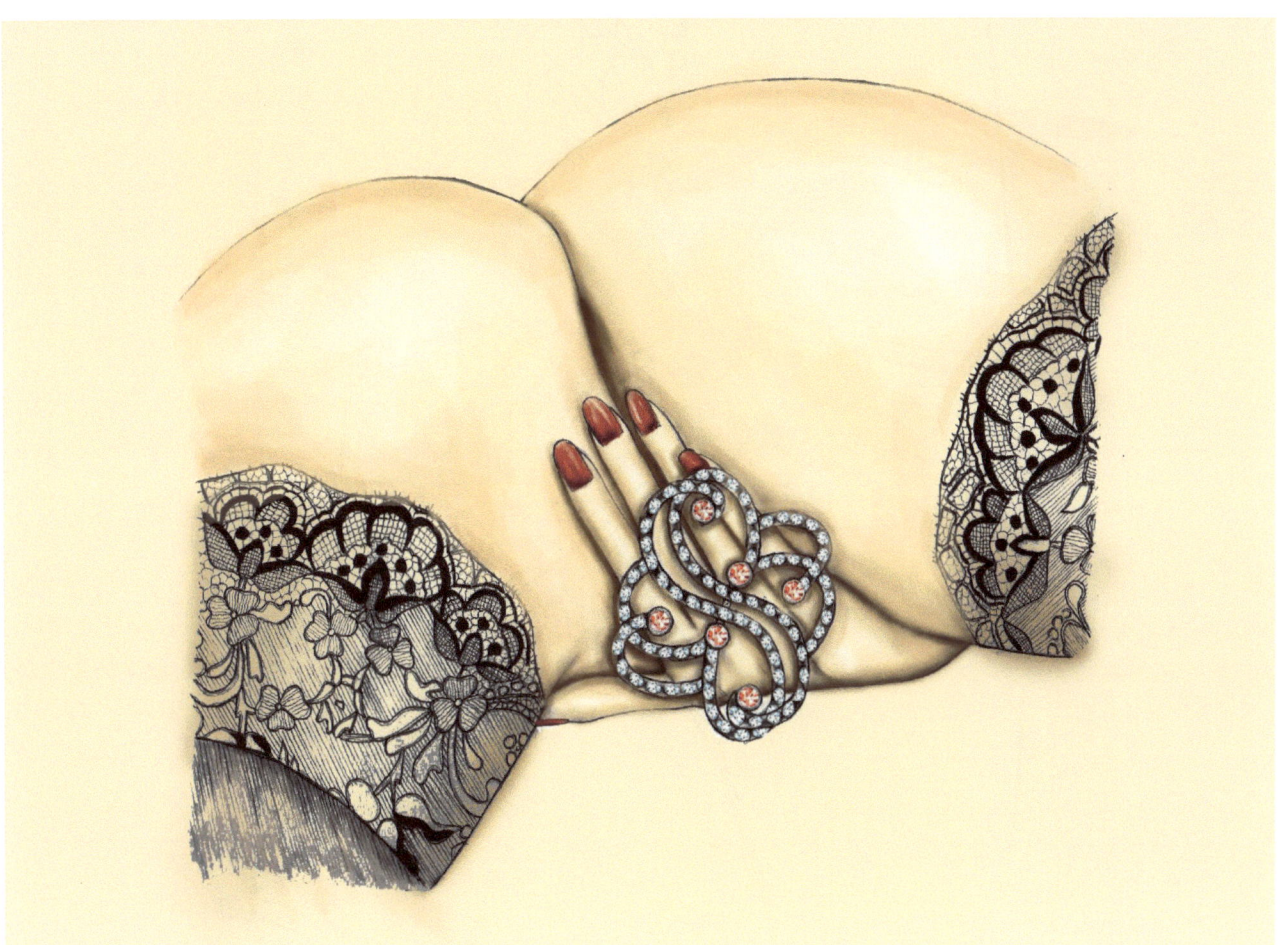

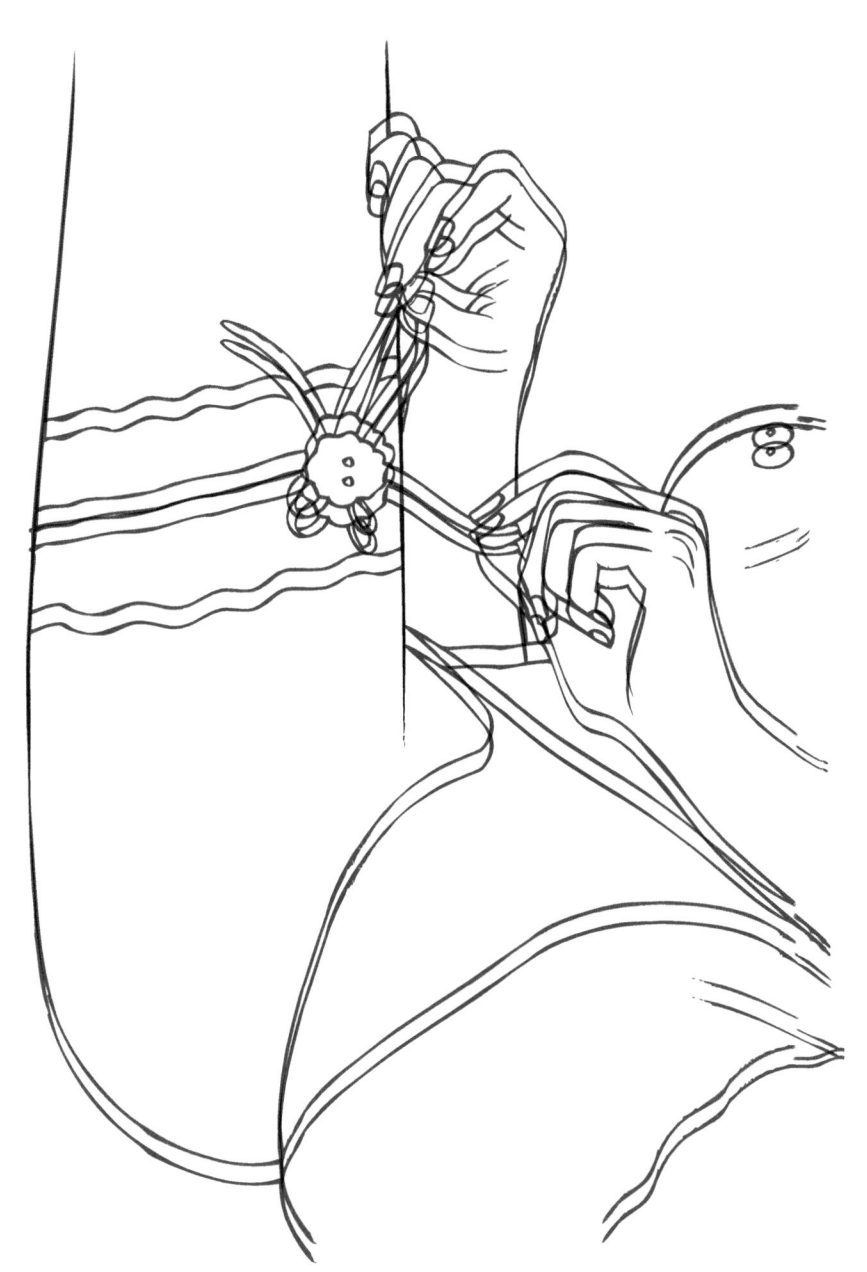

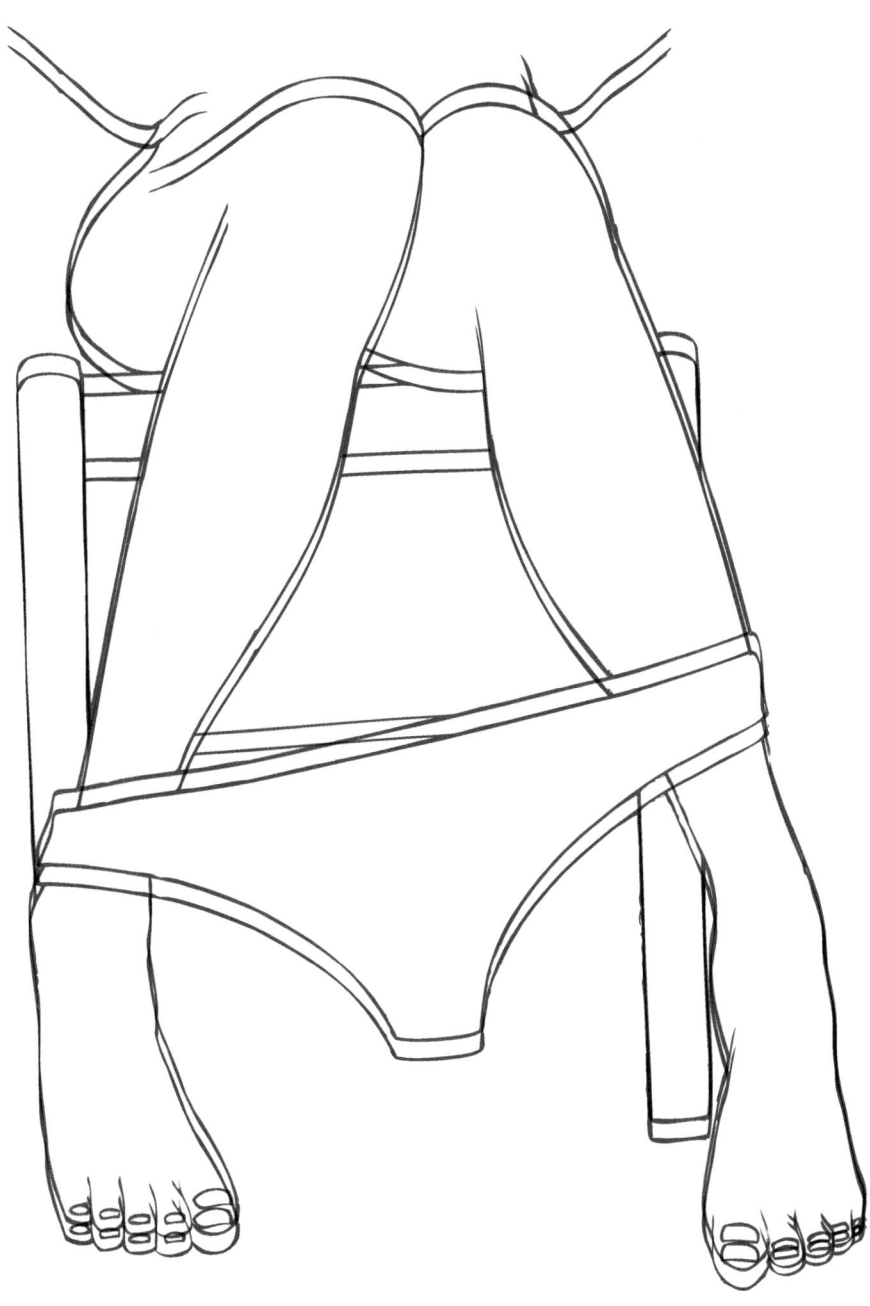

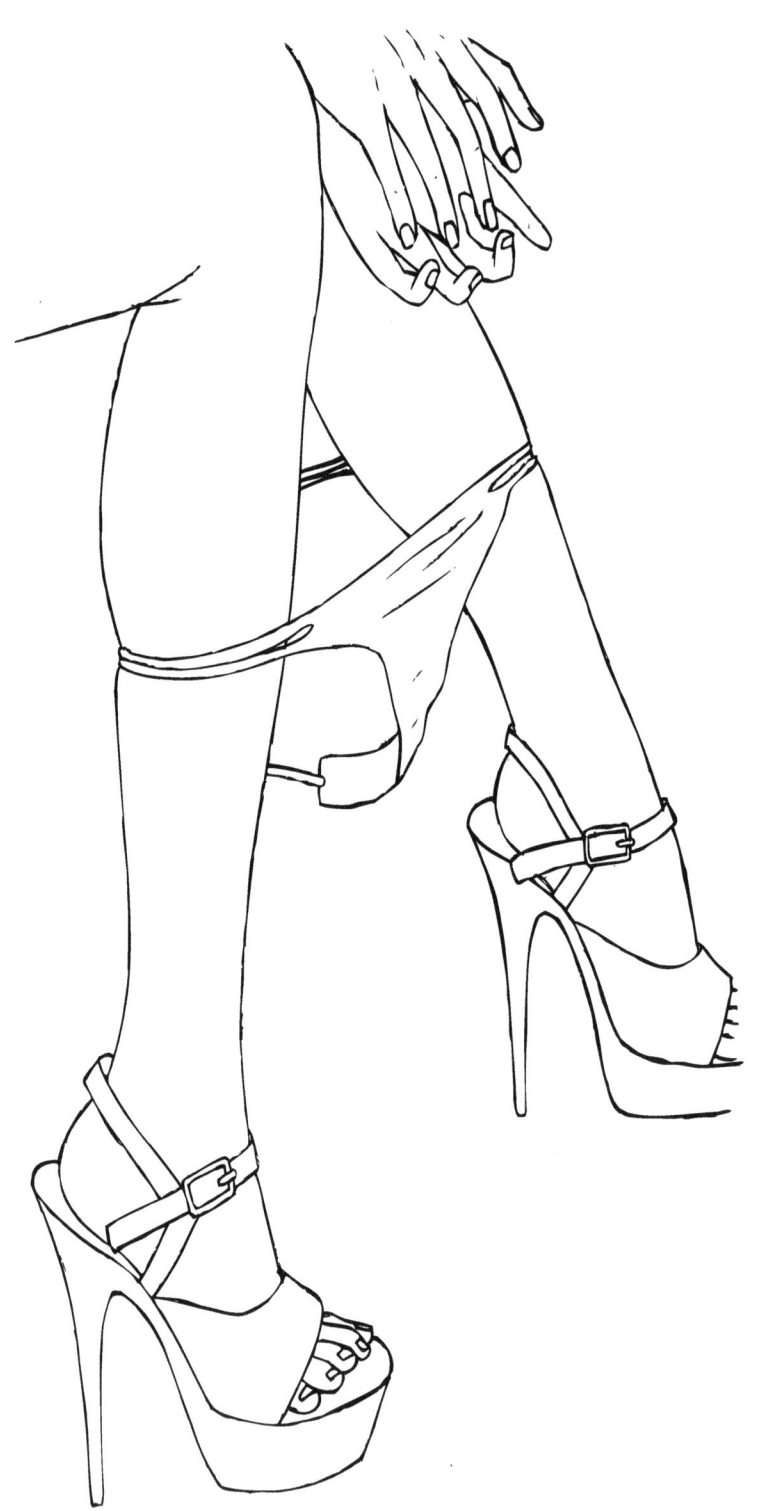

Milan Fashion Campus

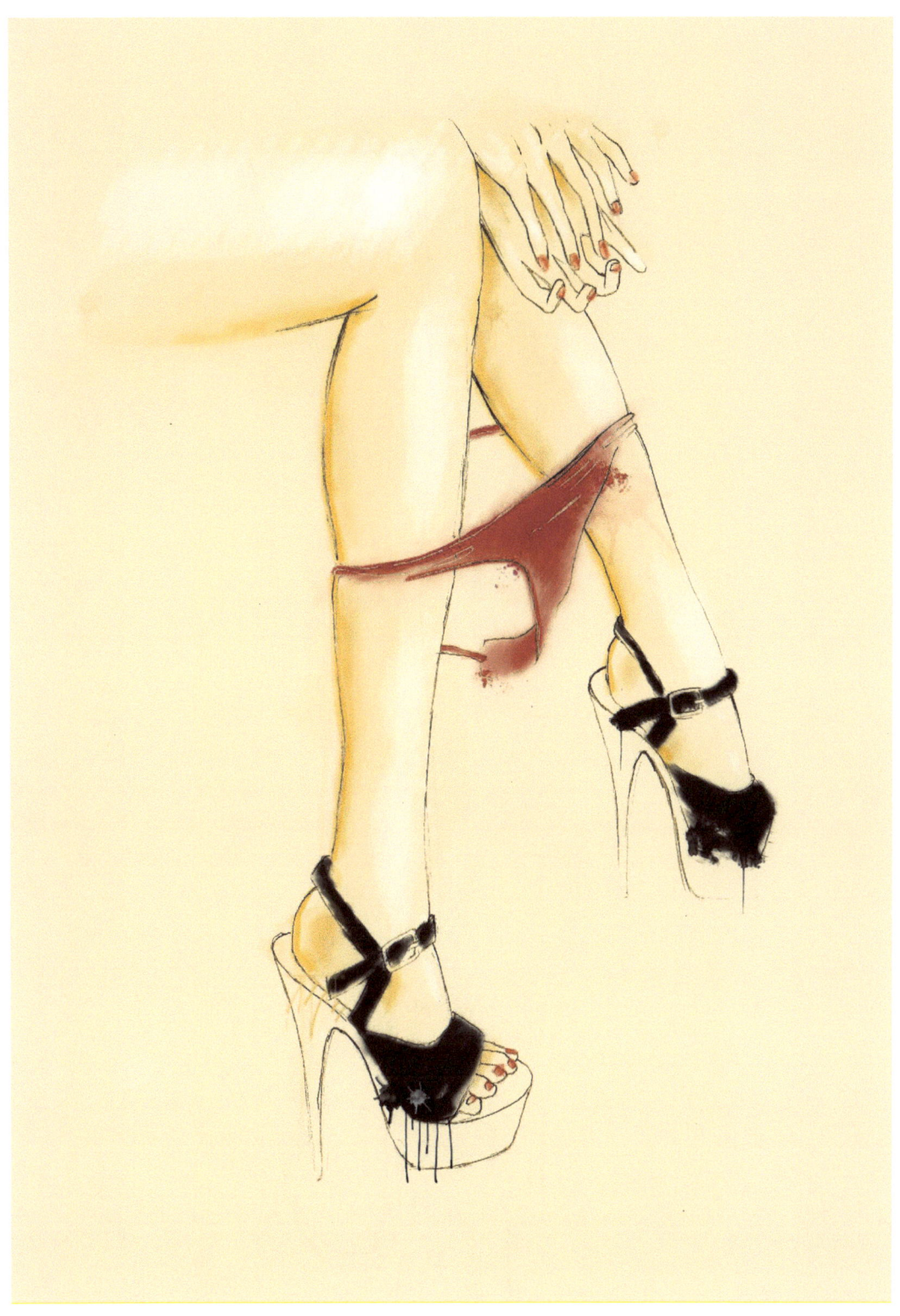

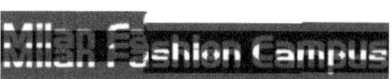
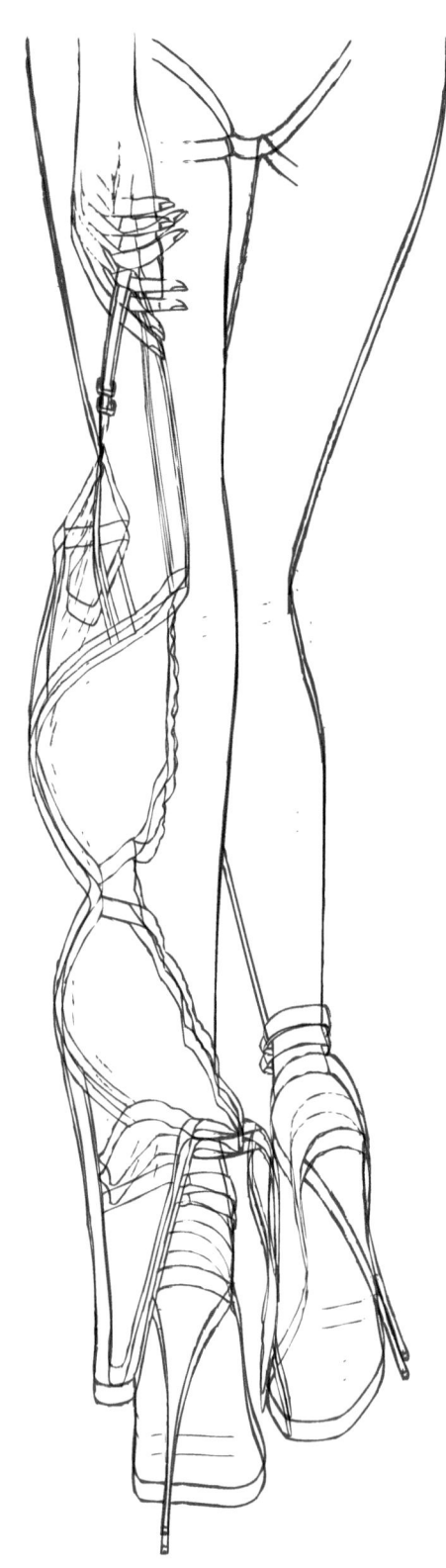

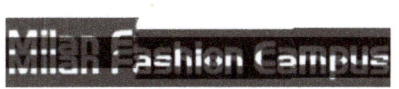

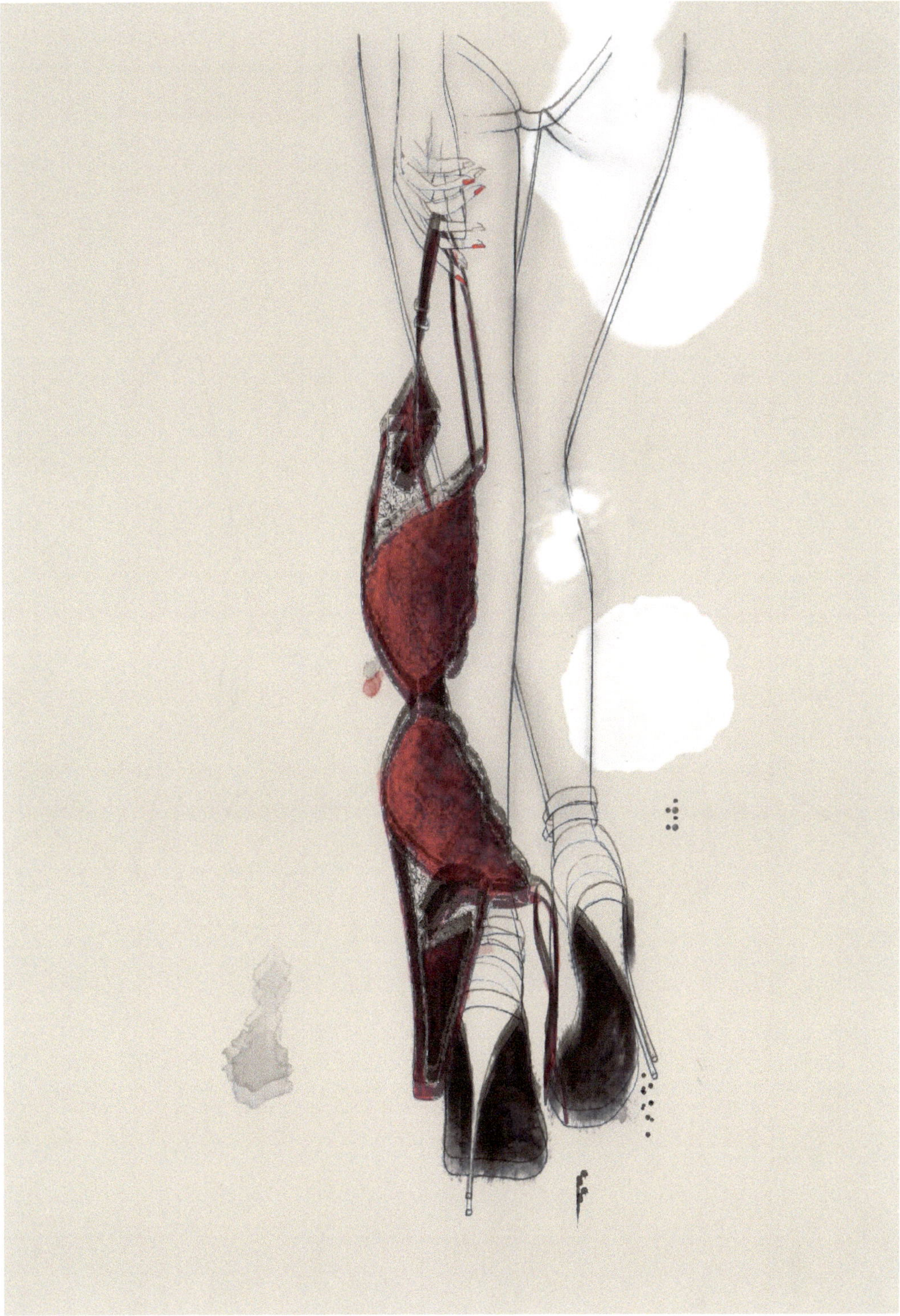

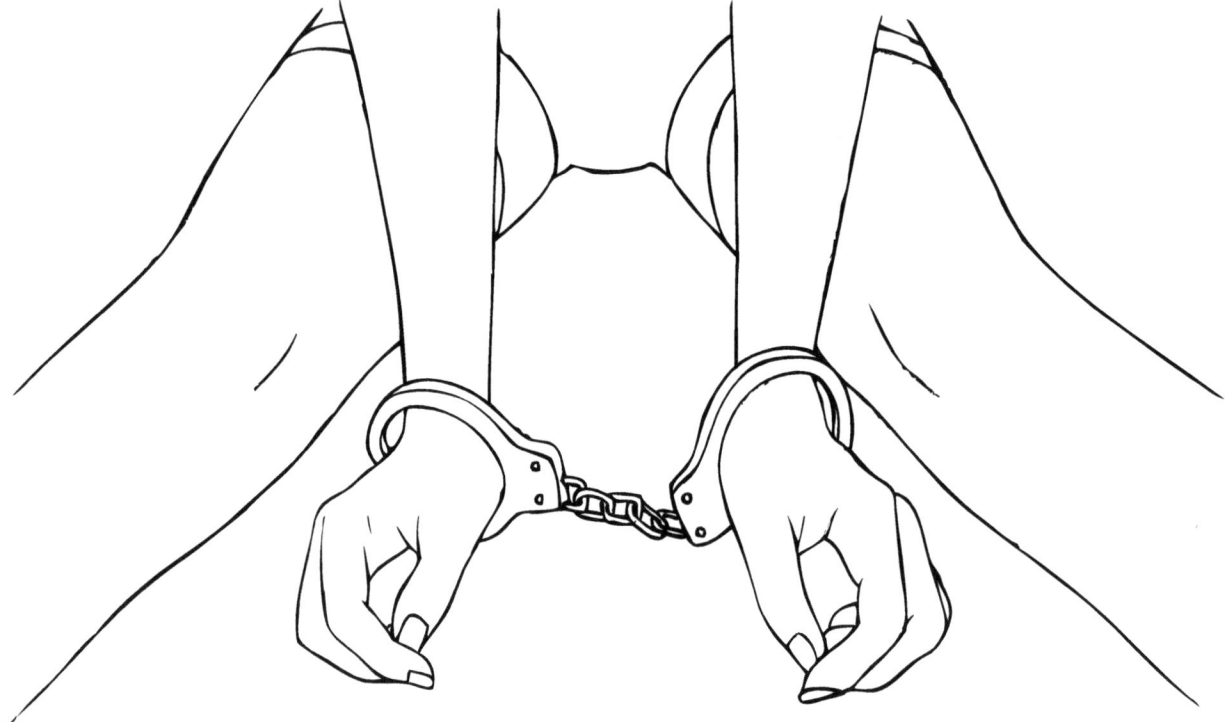

Milan Fashion Campus

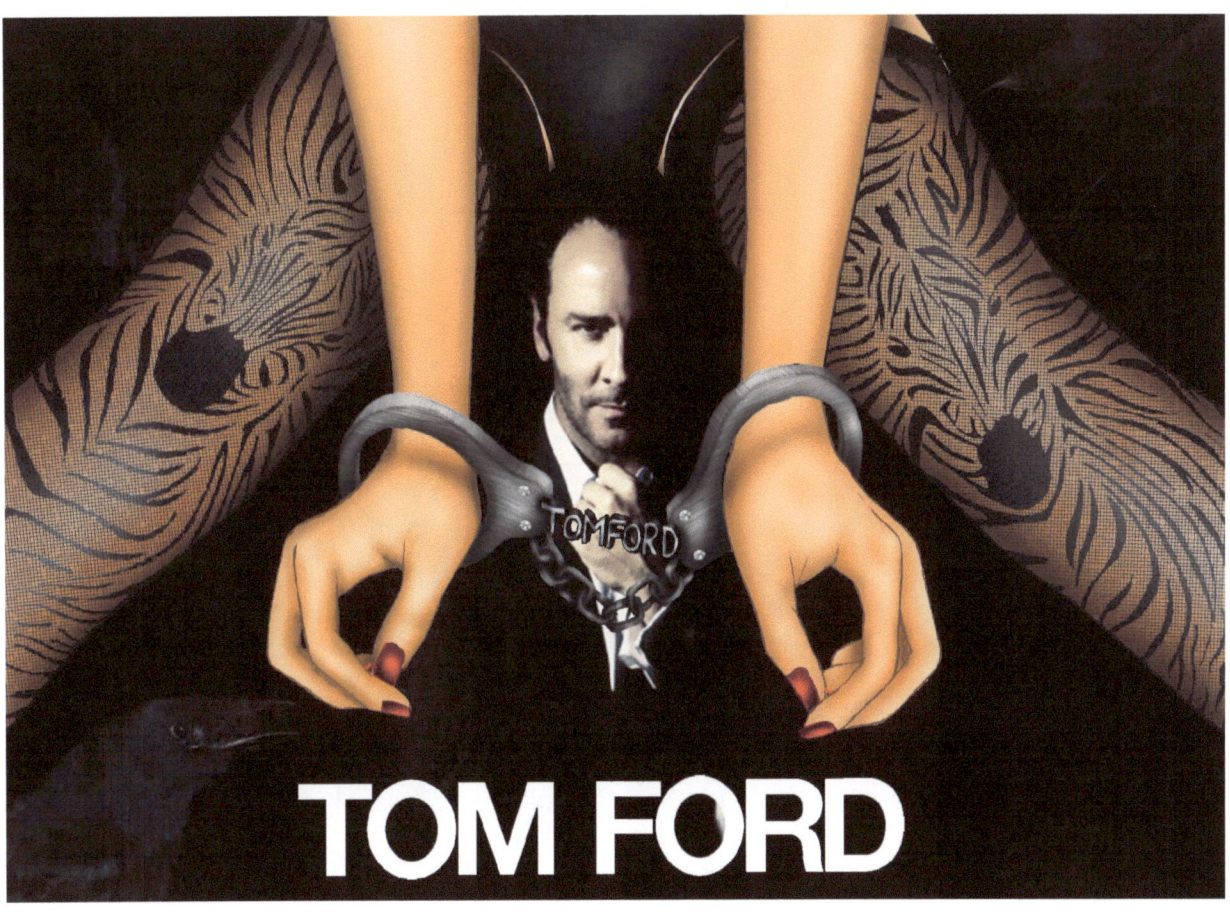

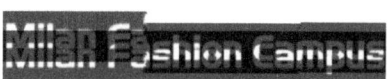

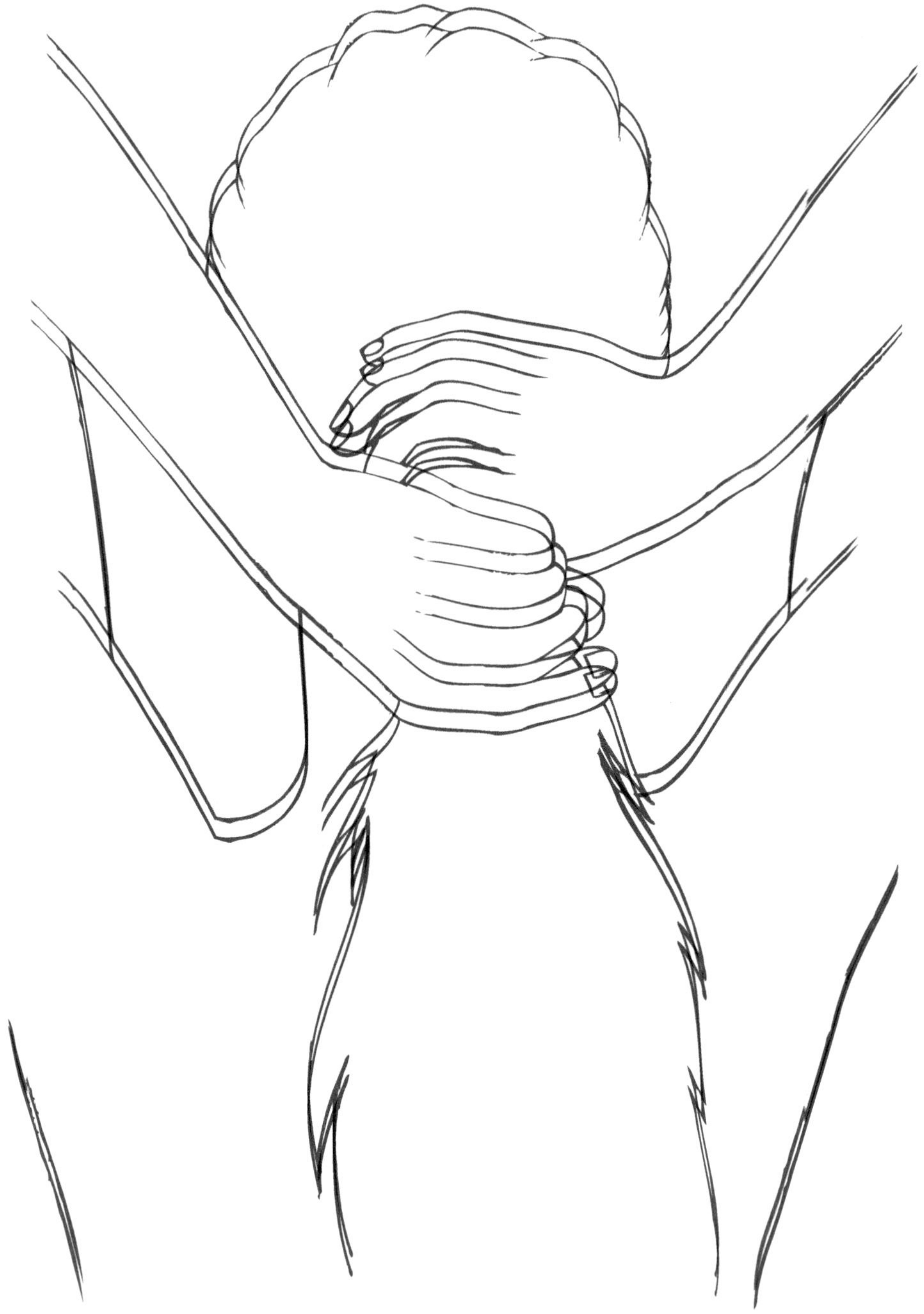

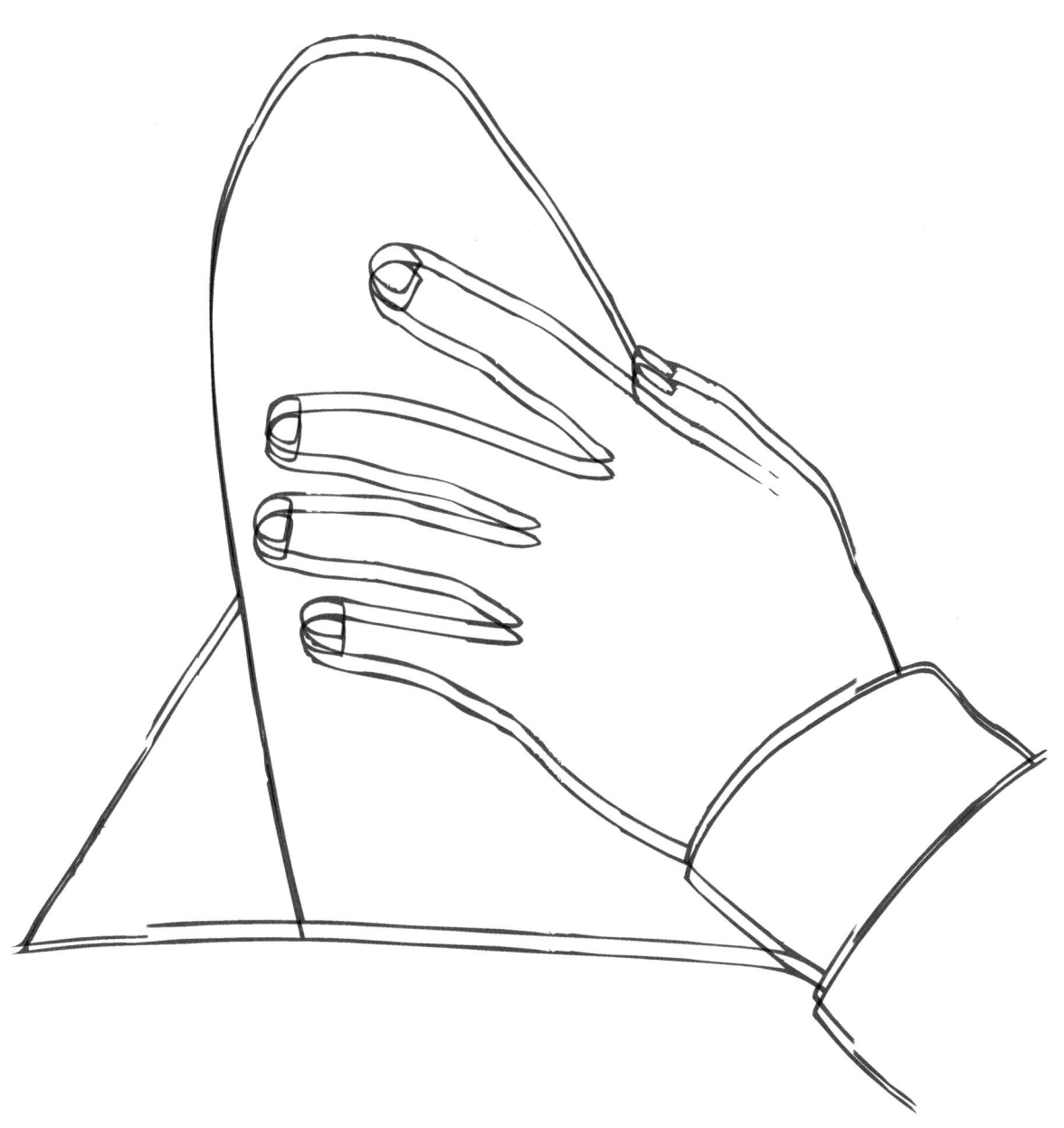

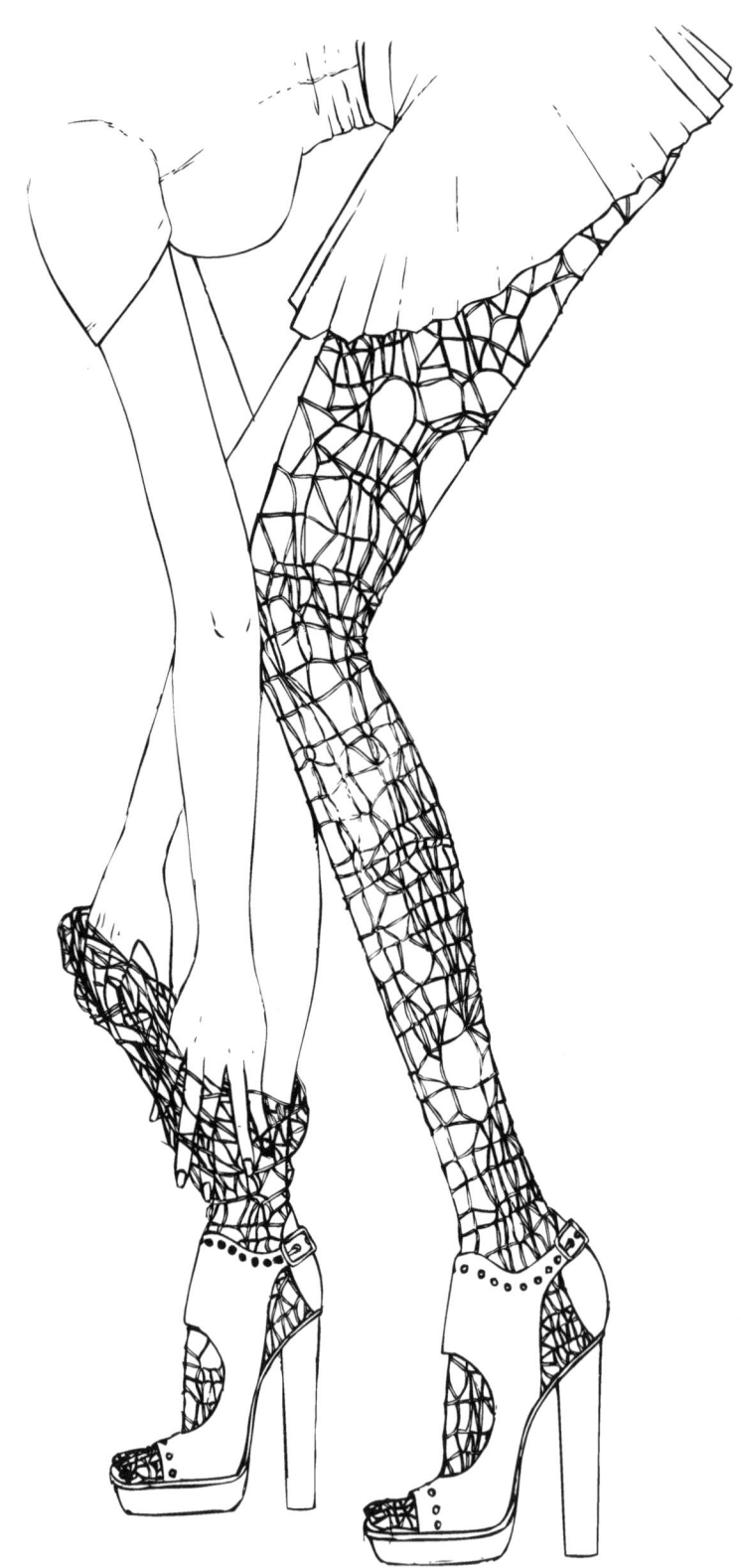

Milan Fashion Campus

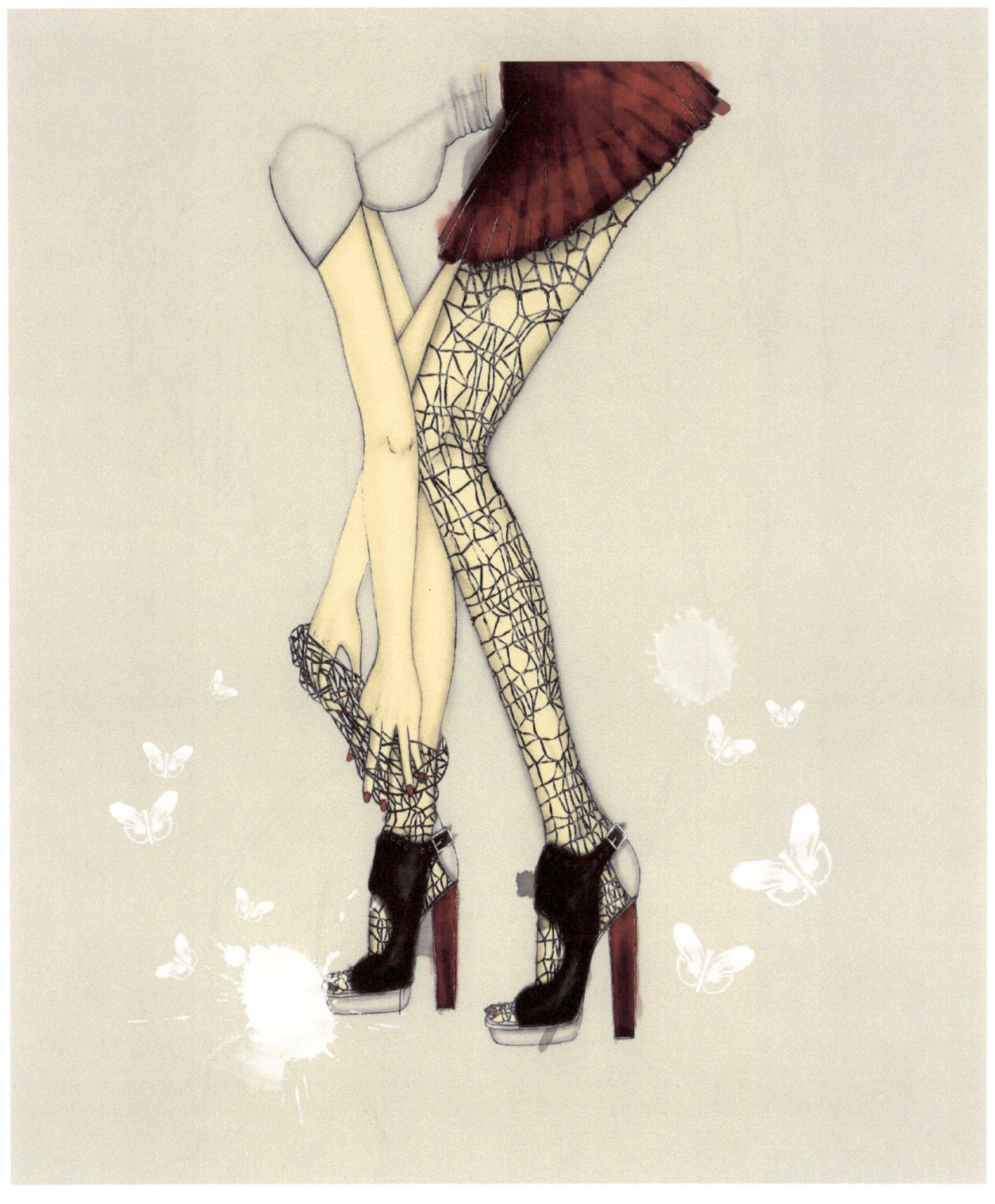

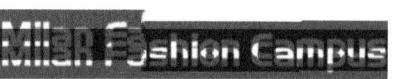

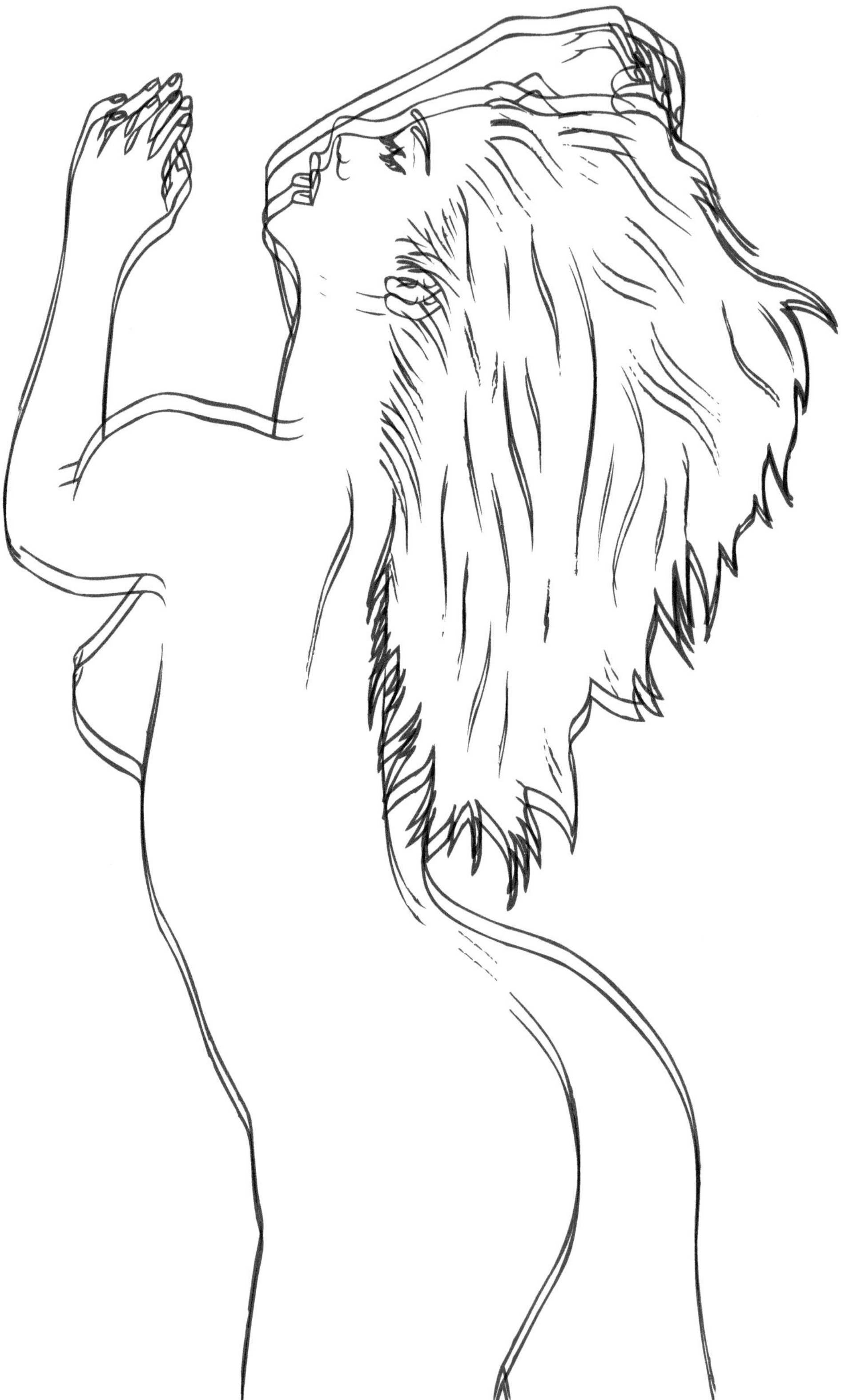

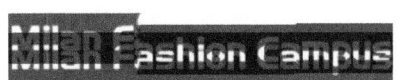

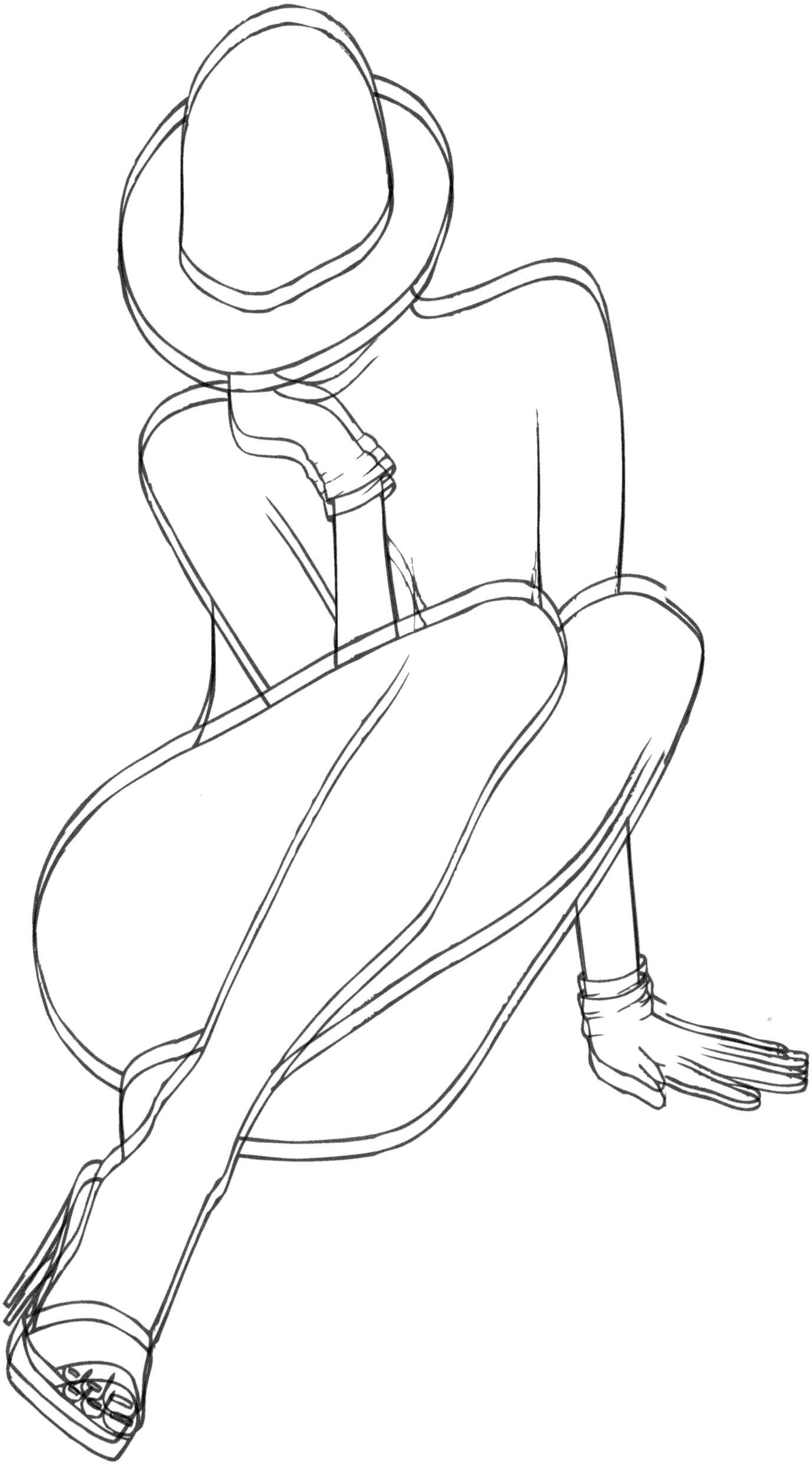

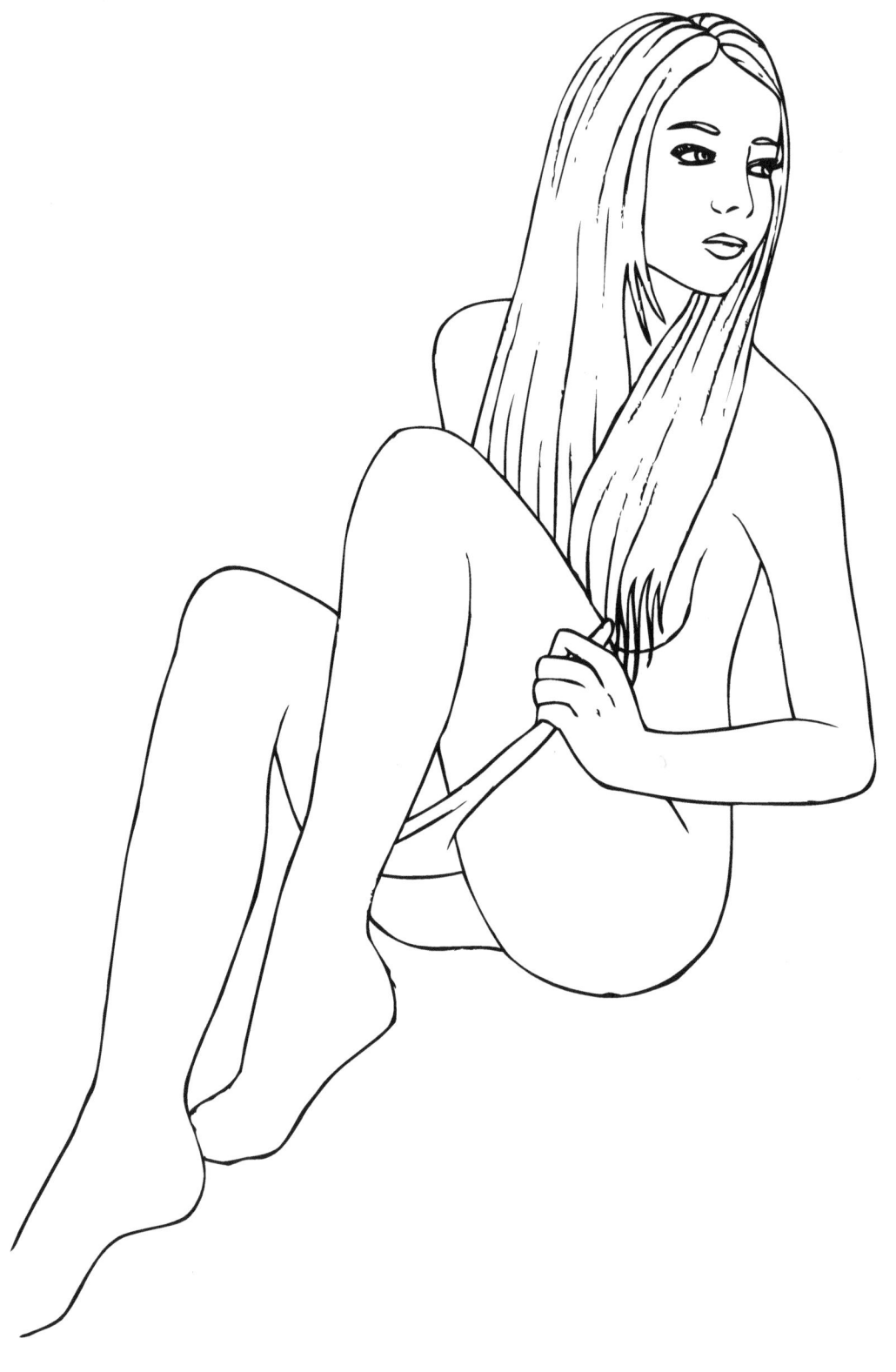

Milan Fashion Campus

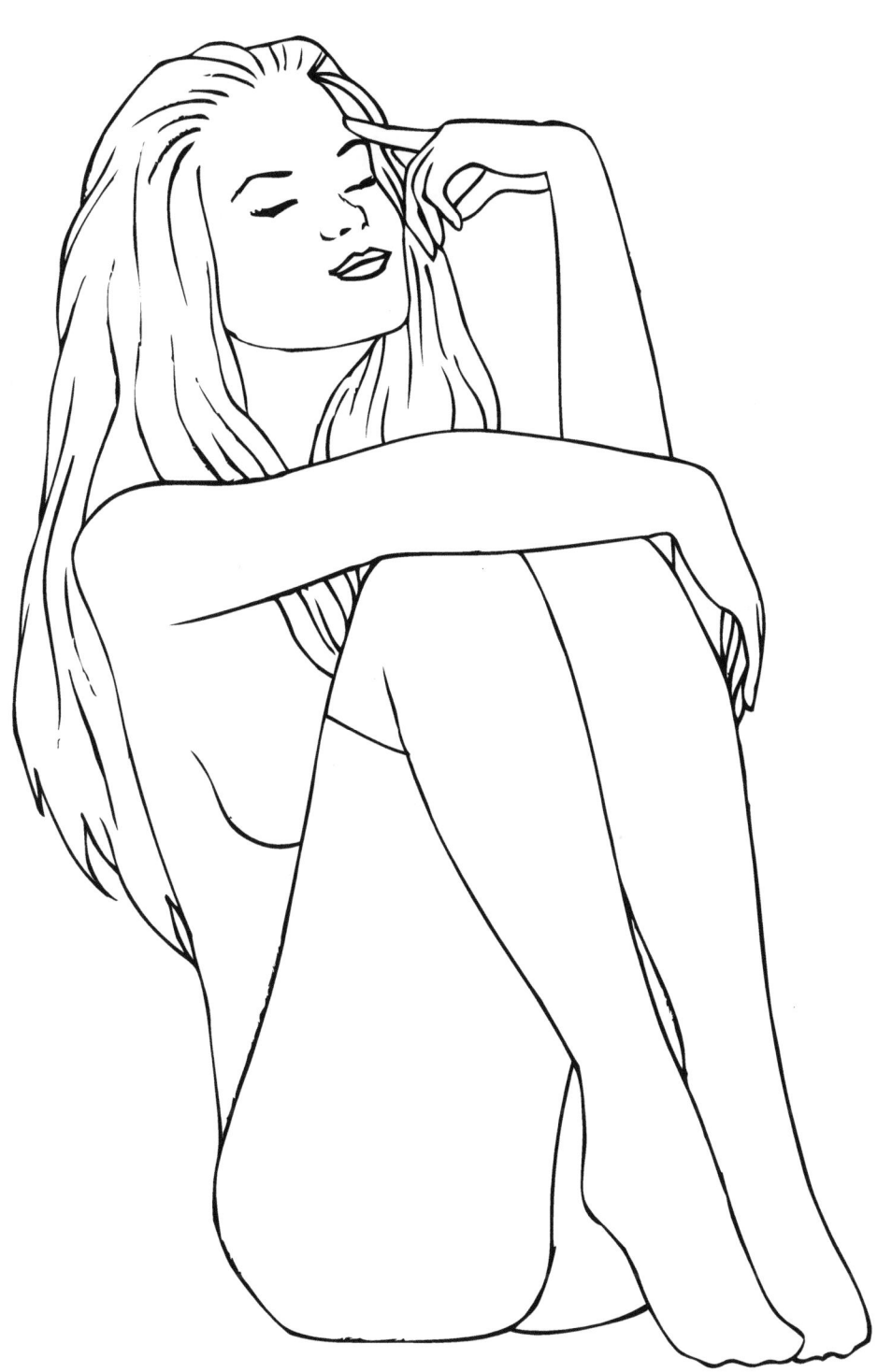

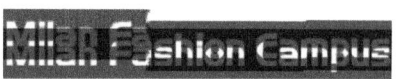

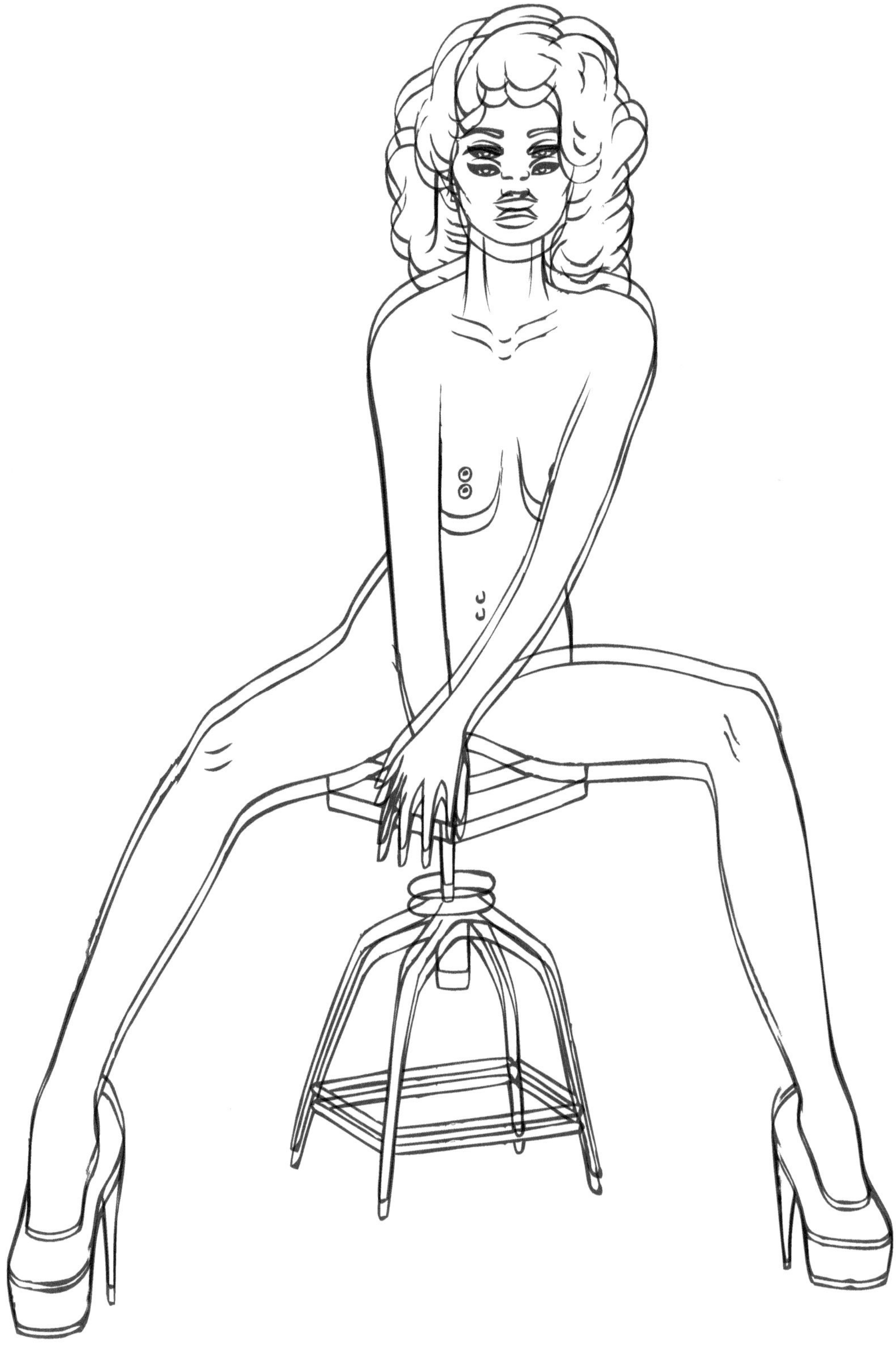

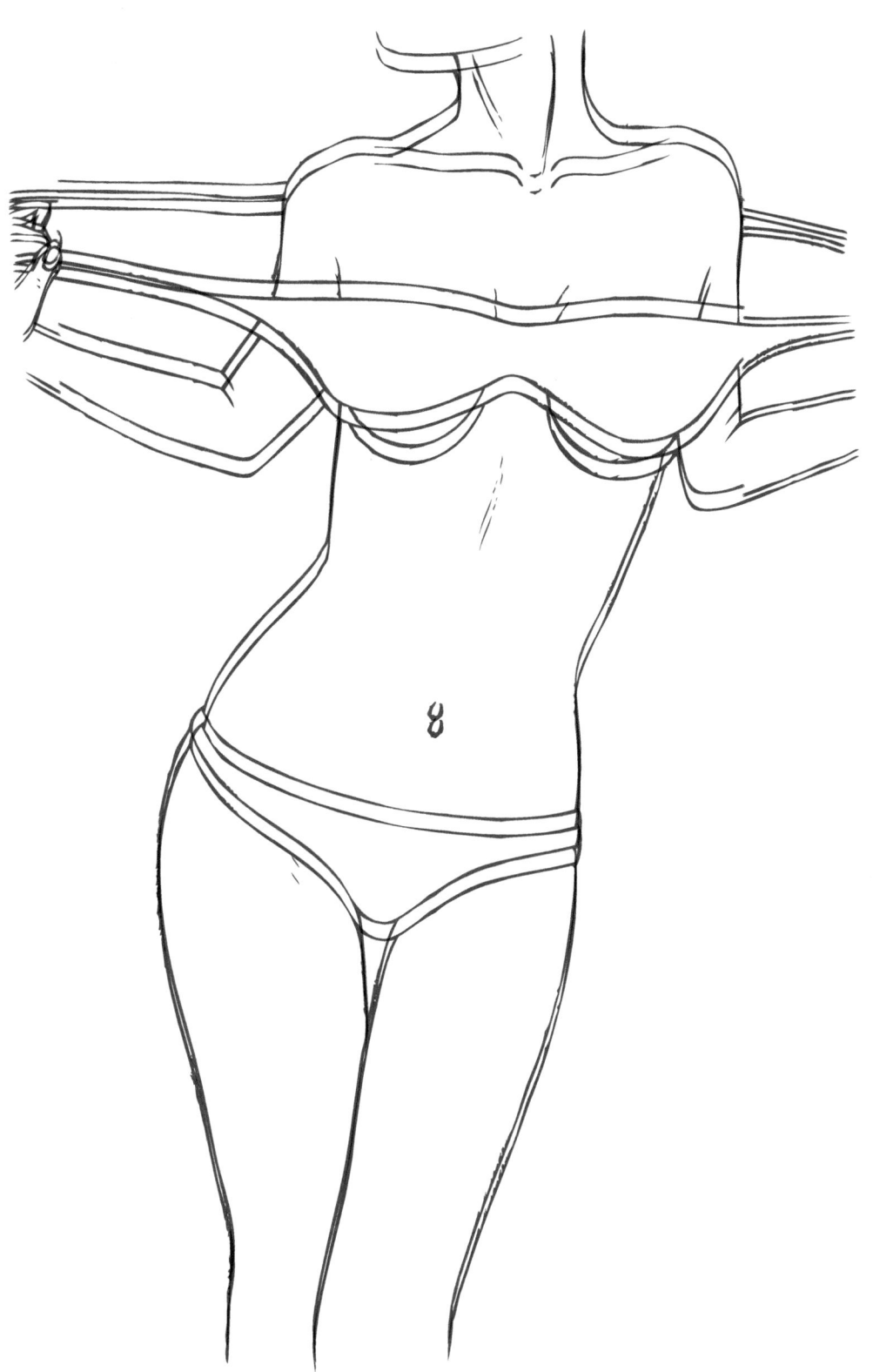

Milan Fashion Campus

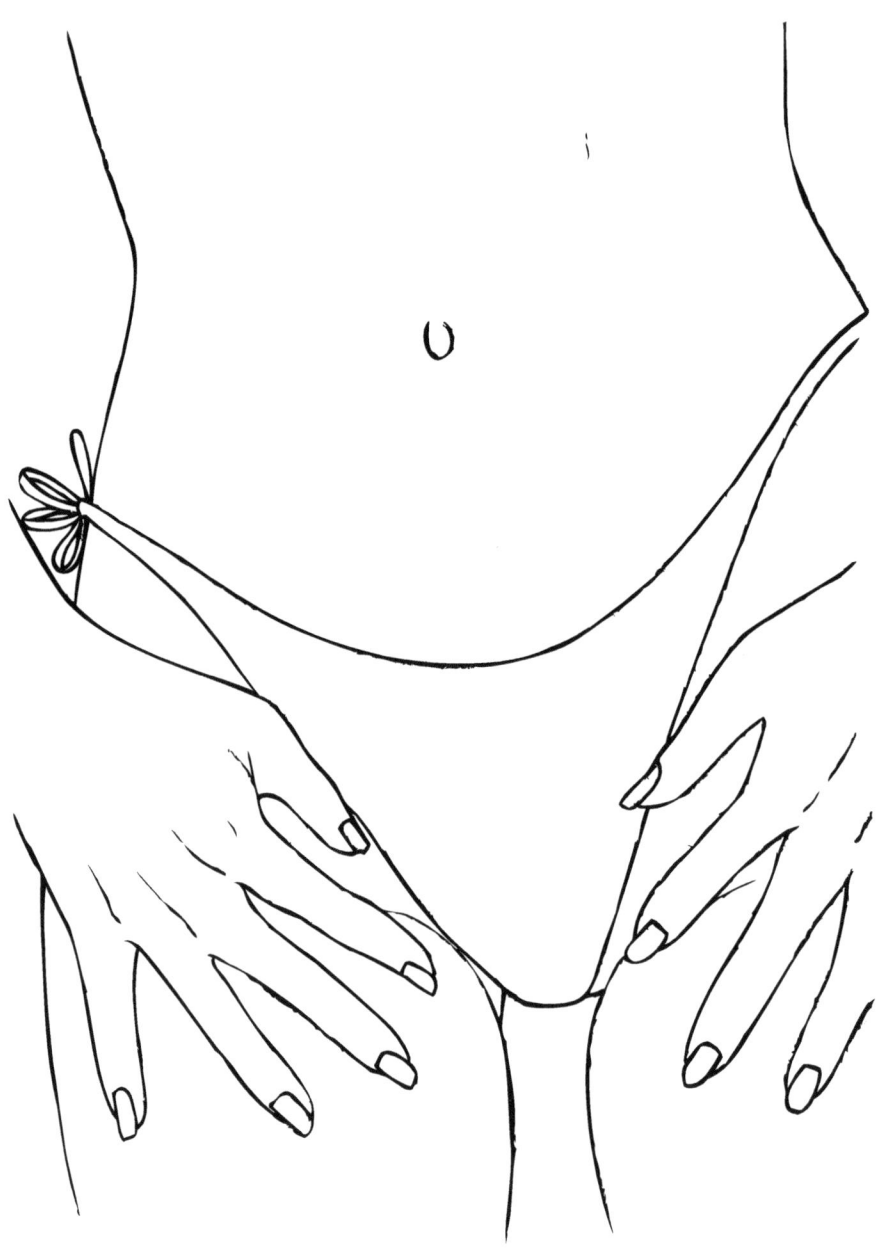

Milan Fashion Campus

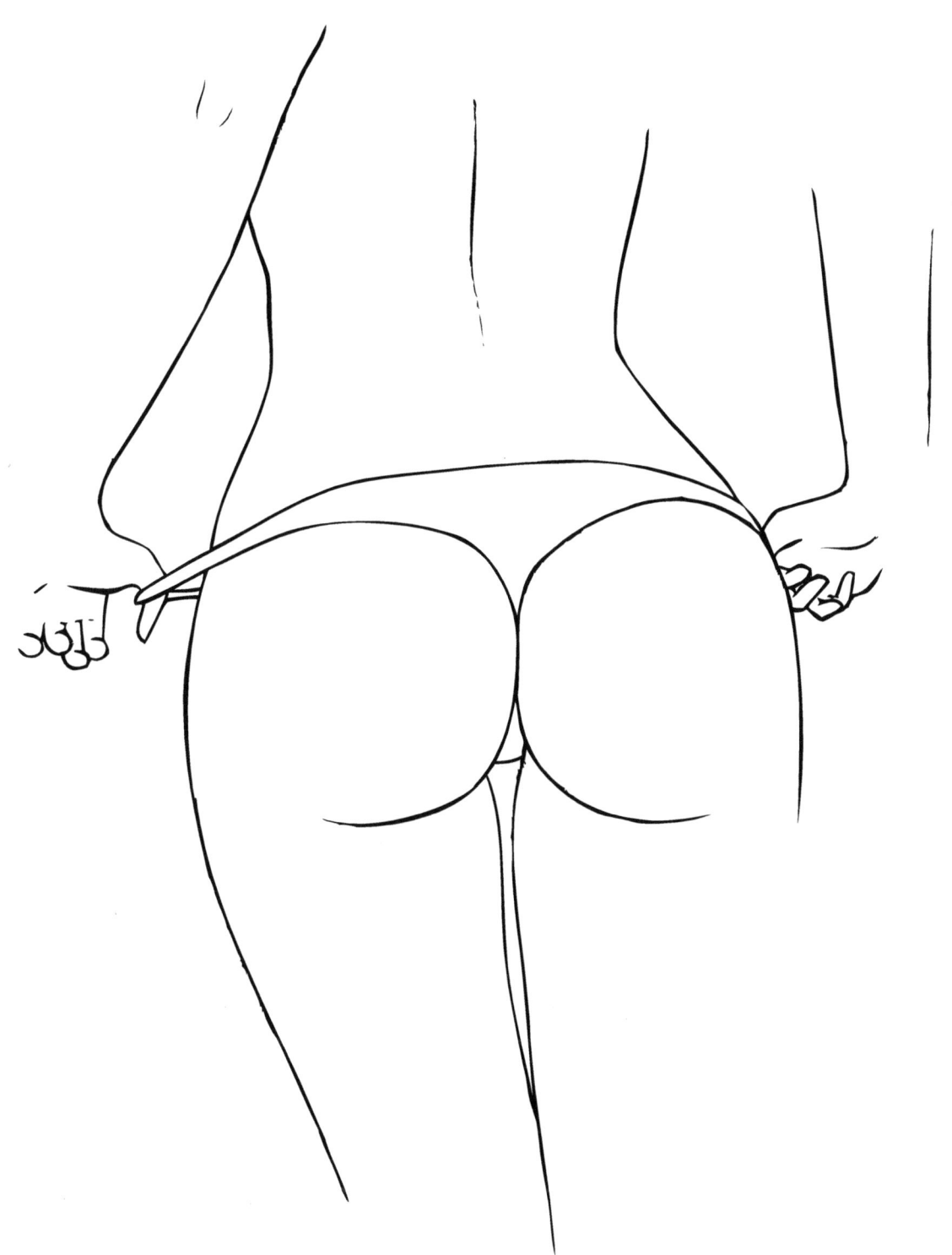

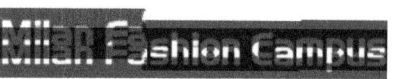

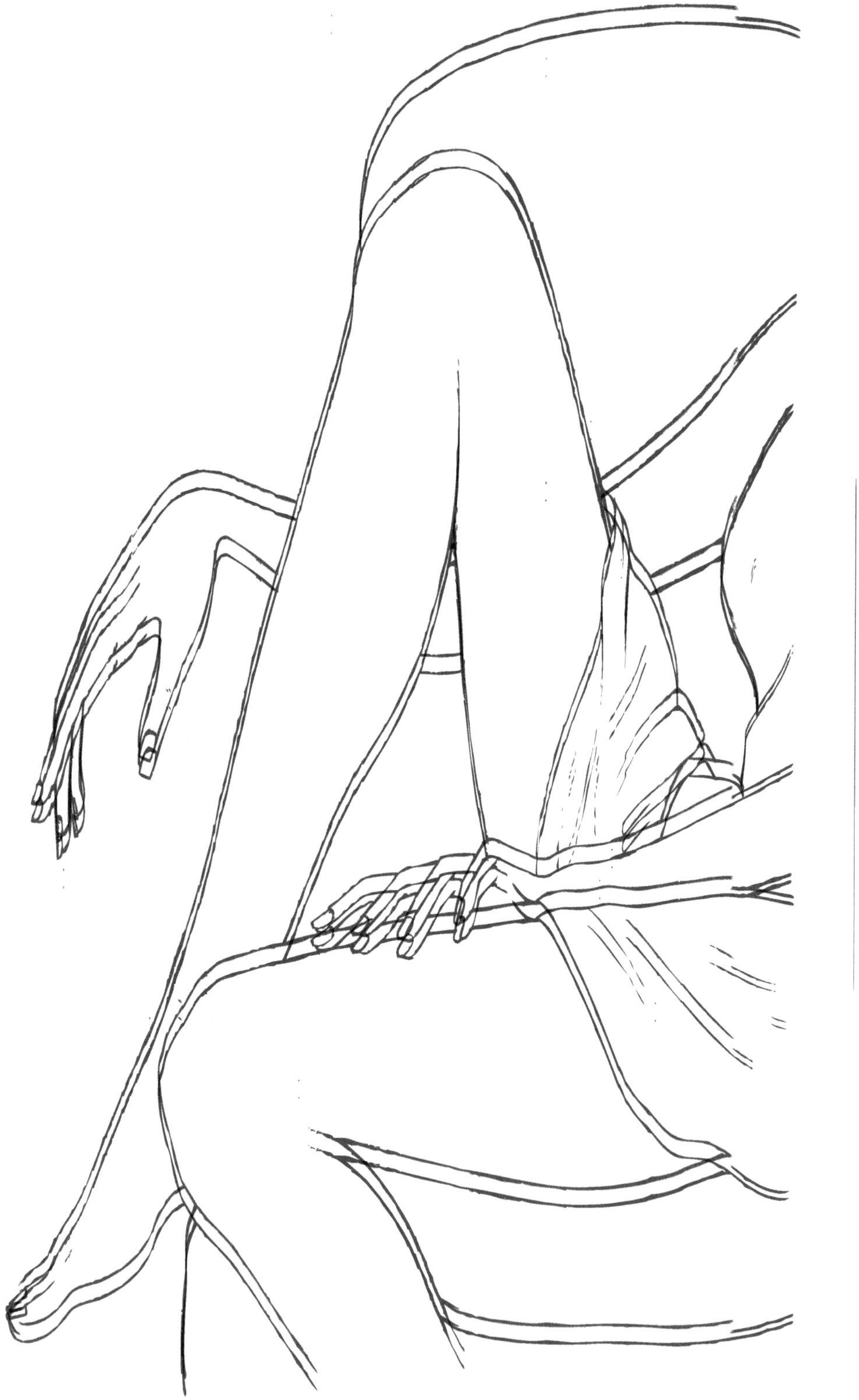

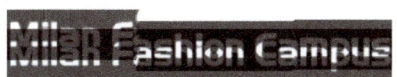

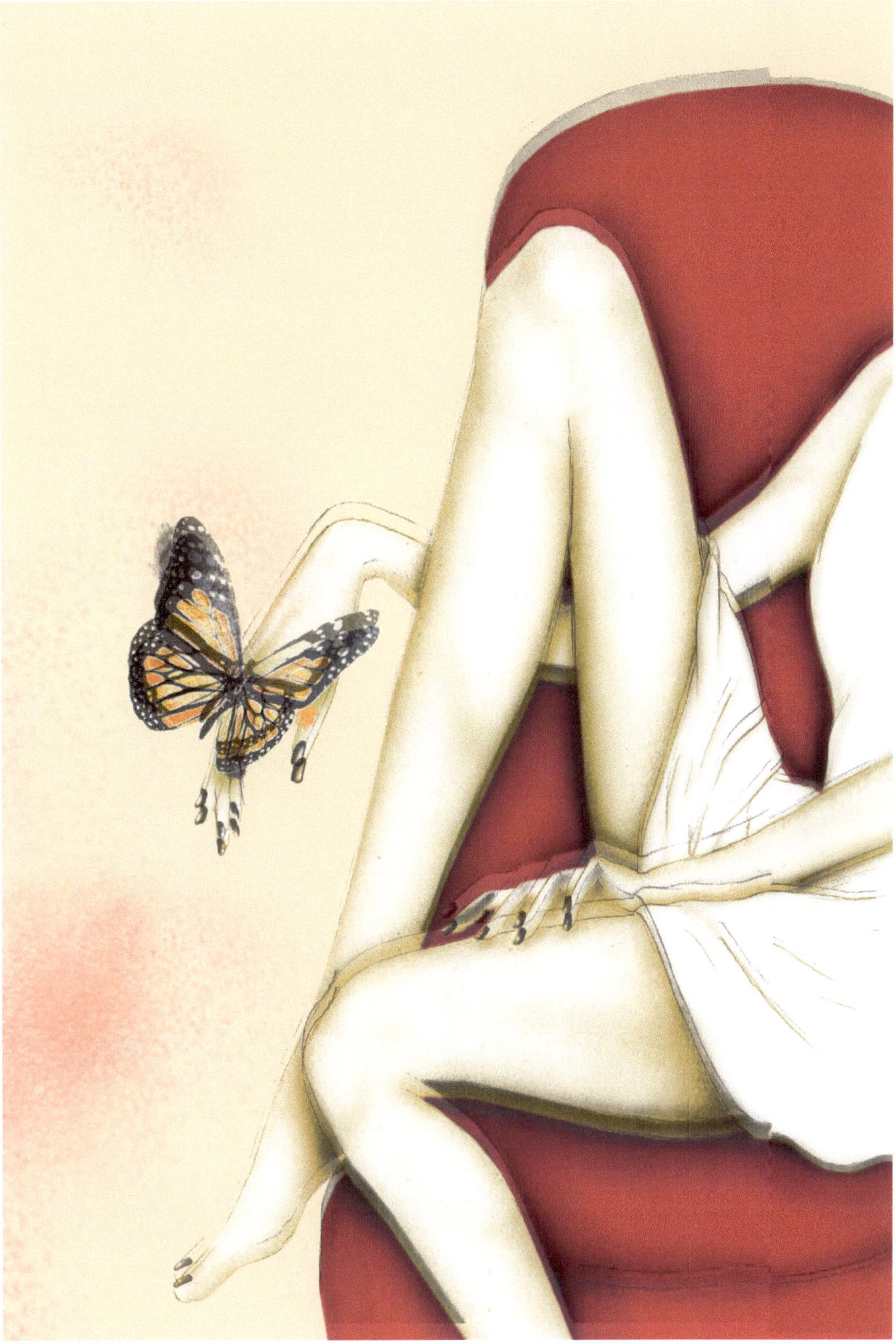

Milan Fashion Campus

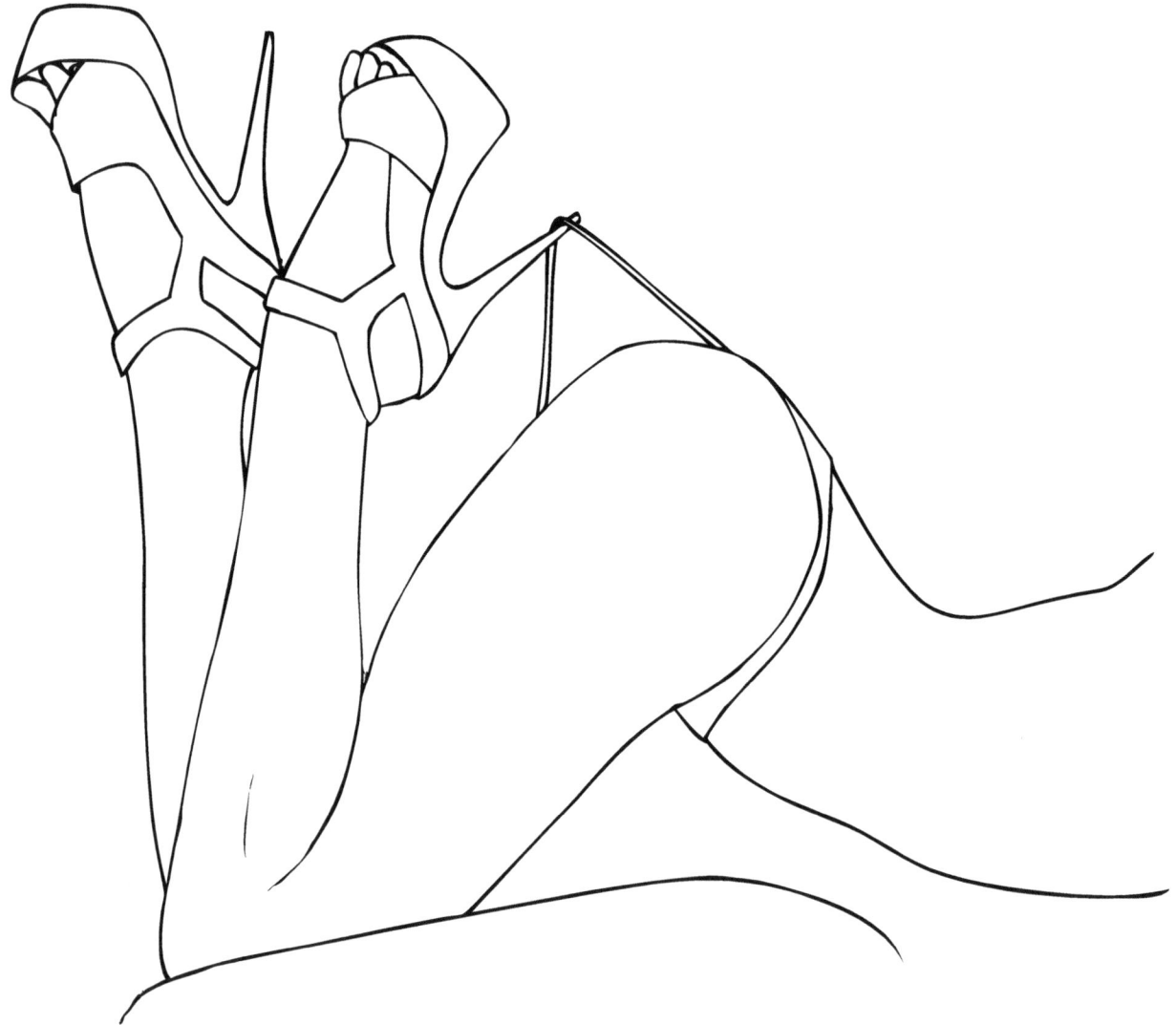

Milan Fashion Campus

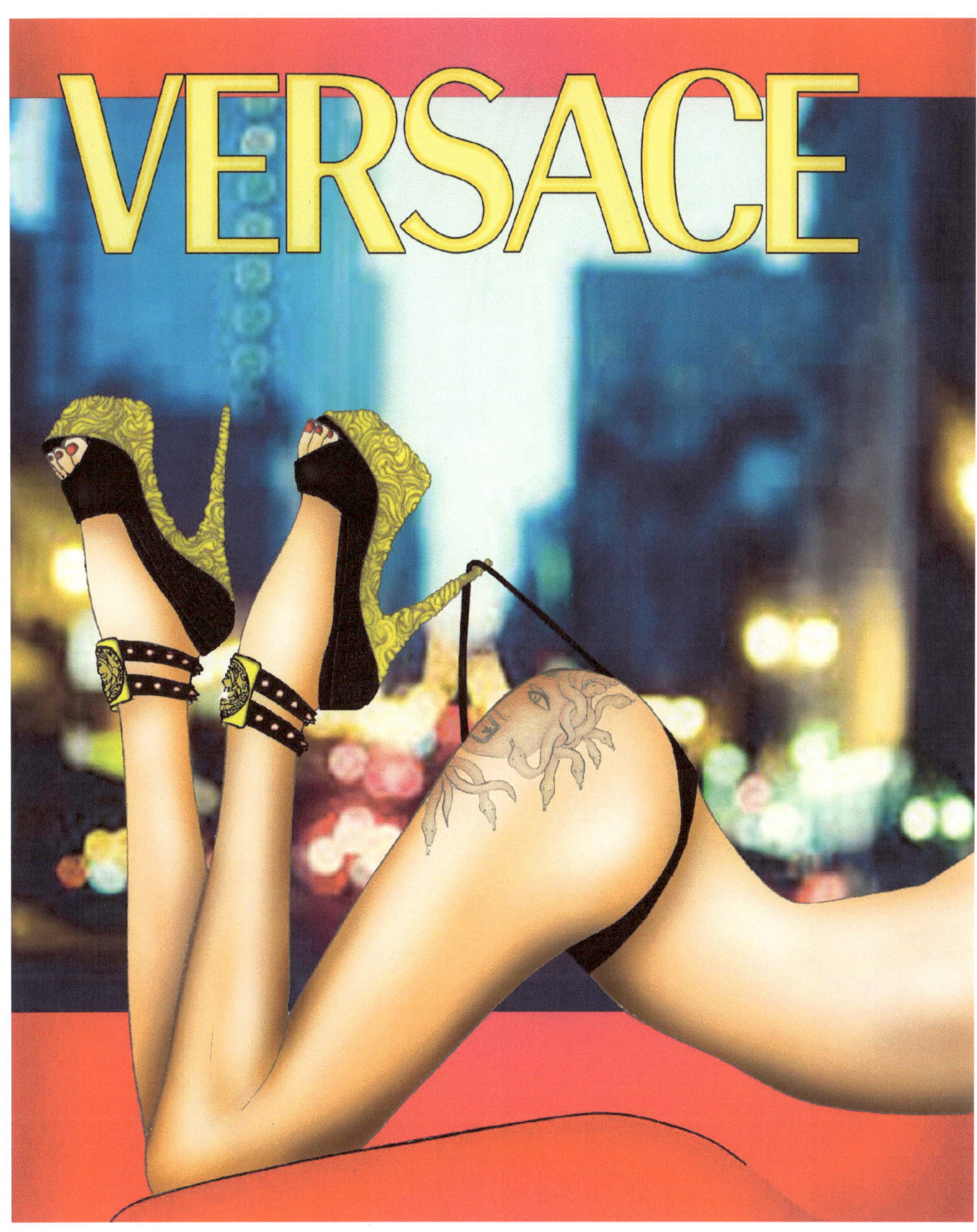

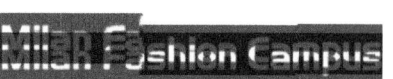

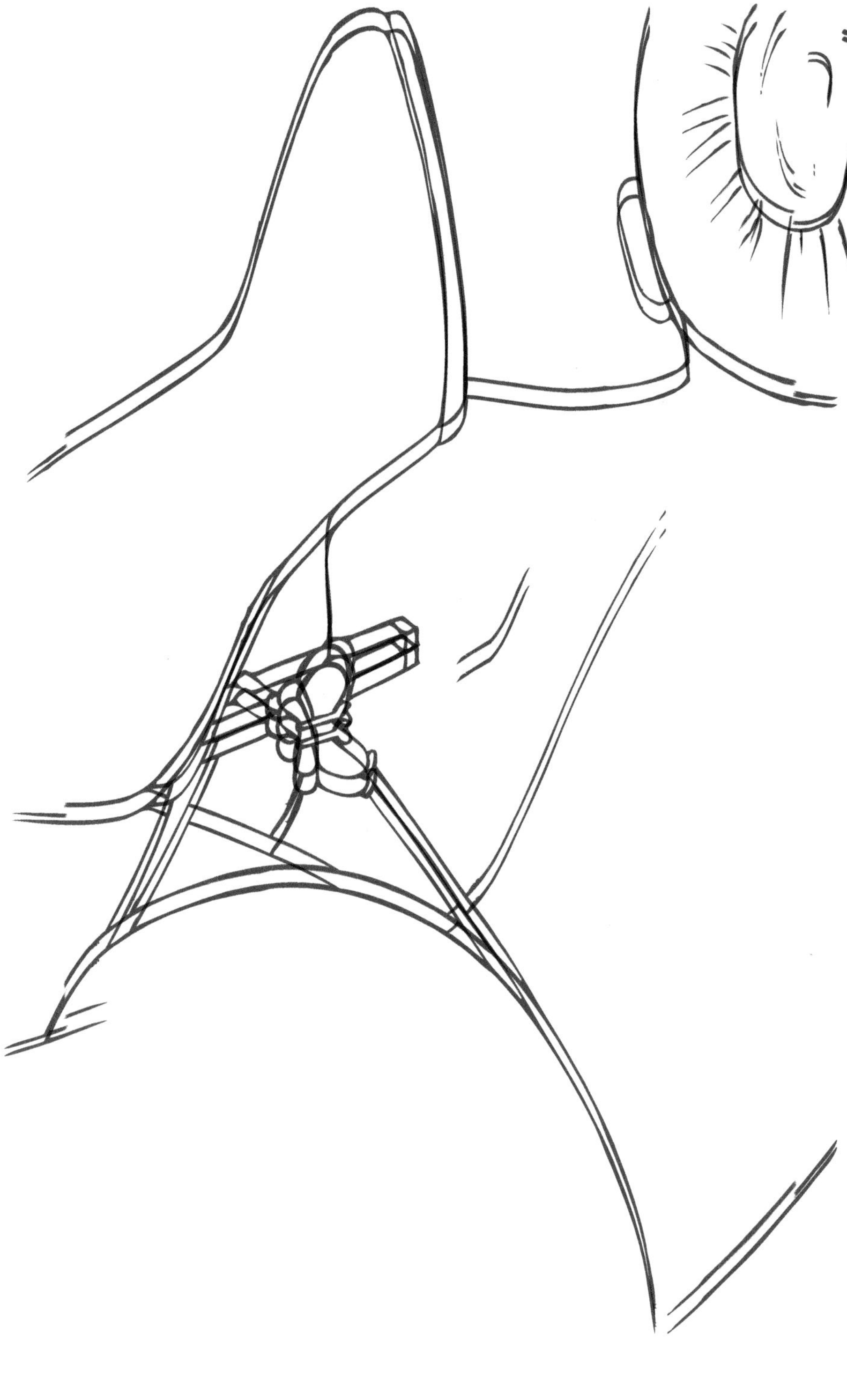

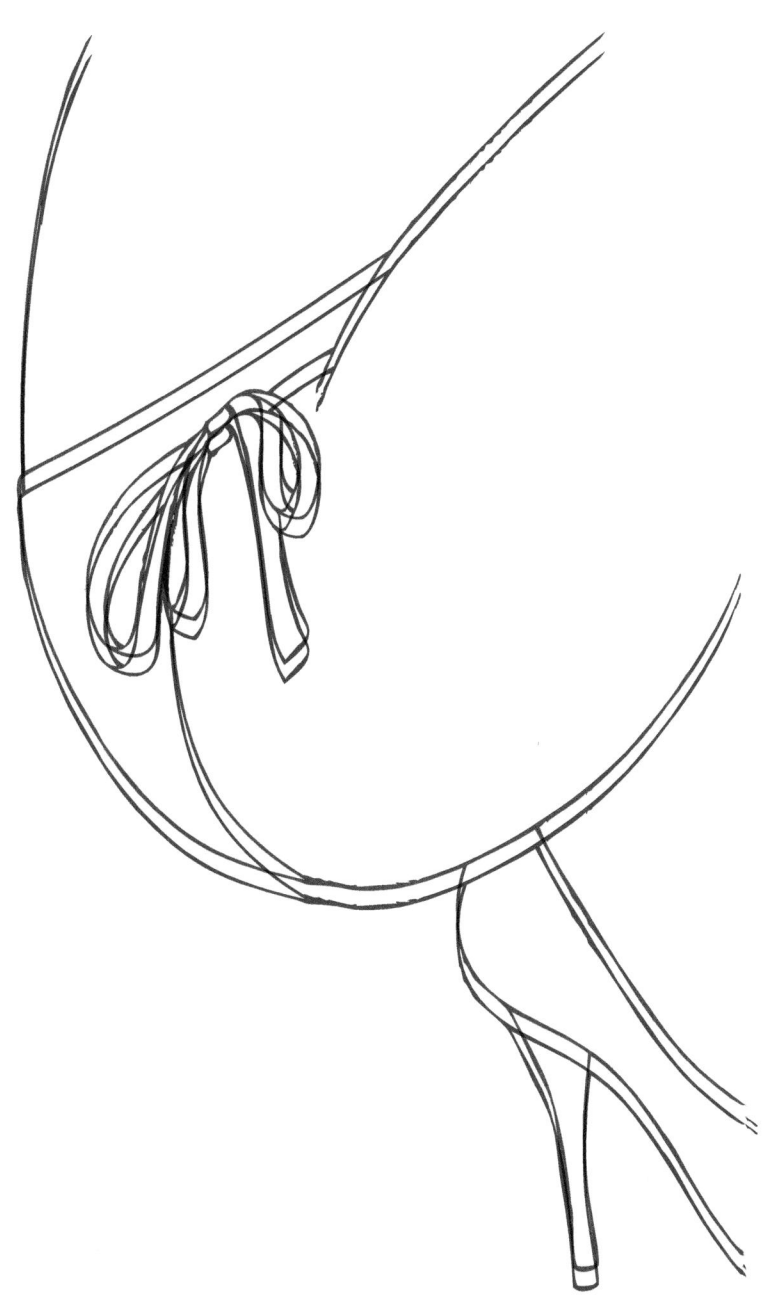

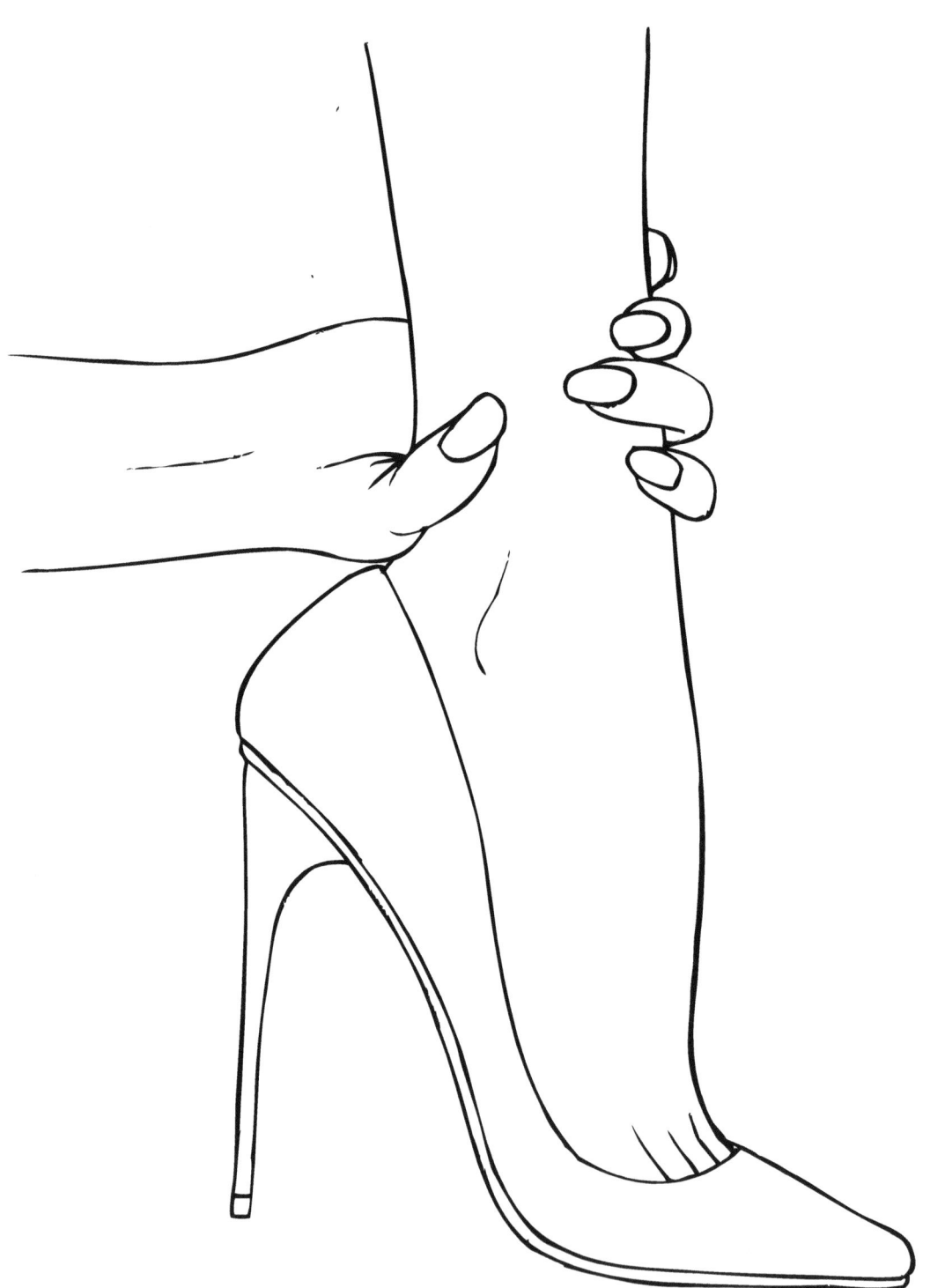

Milan Fashion Campus

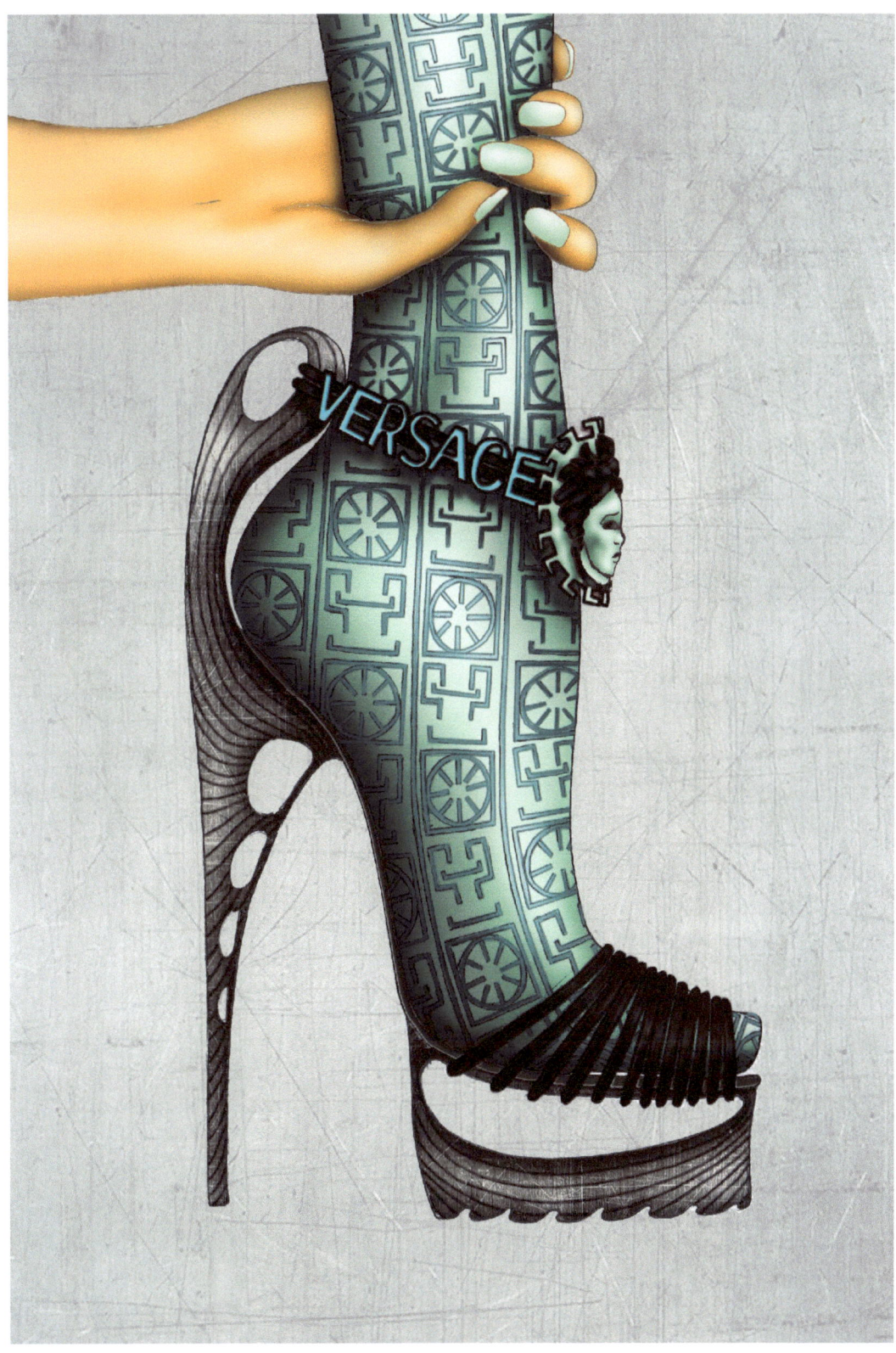

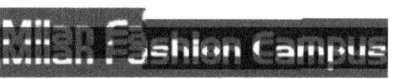

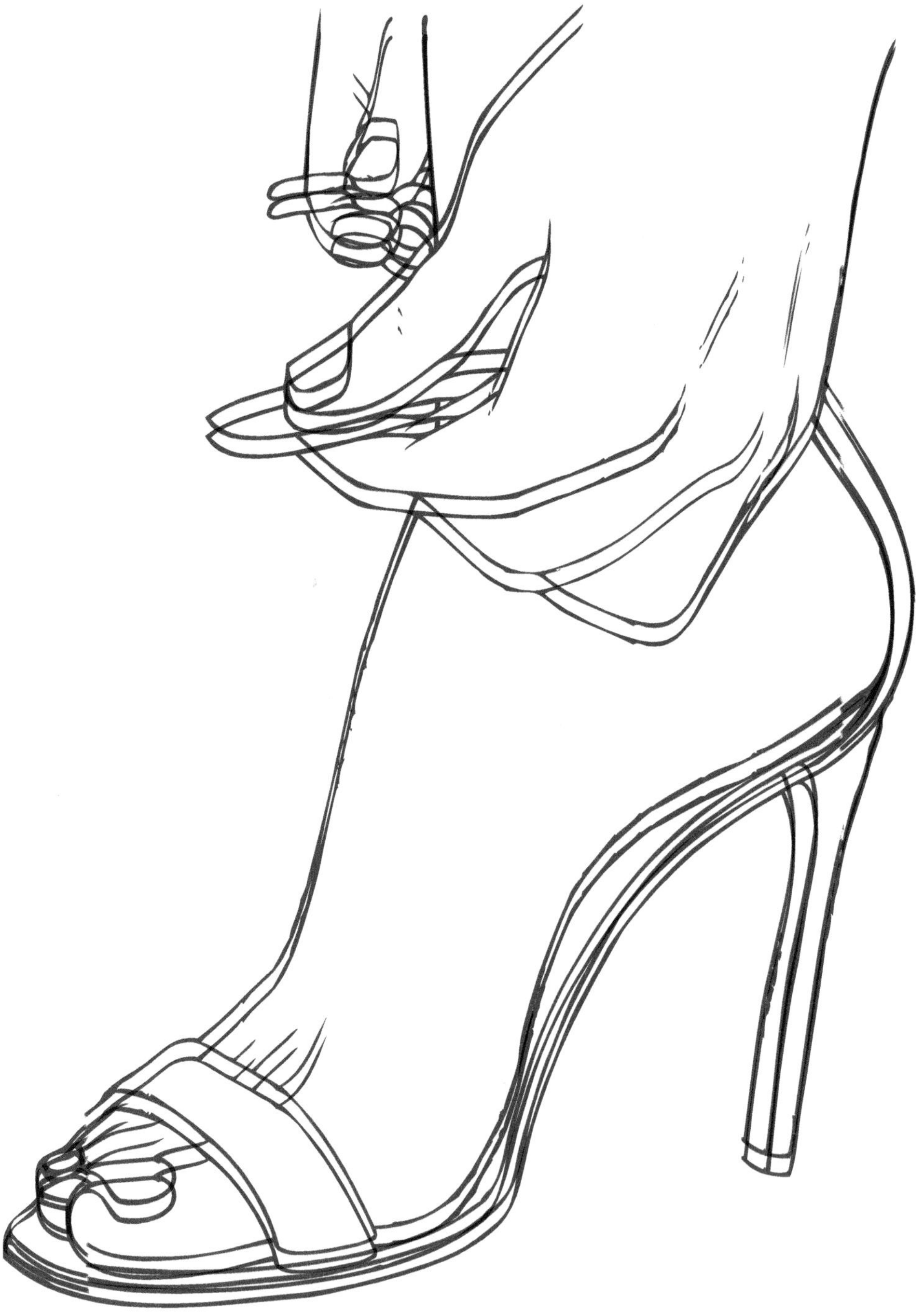

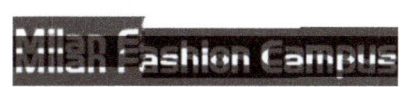

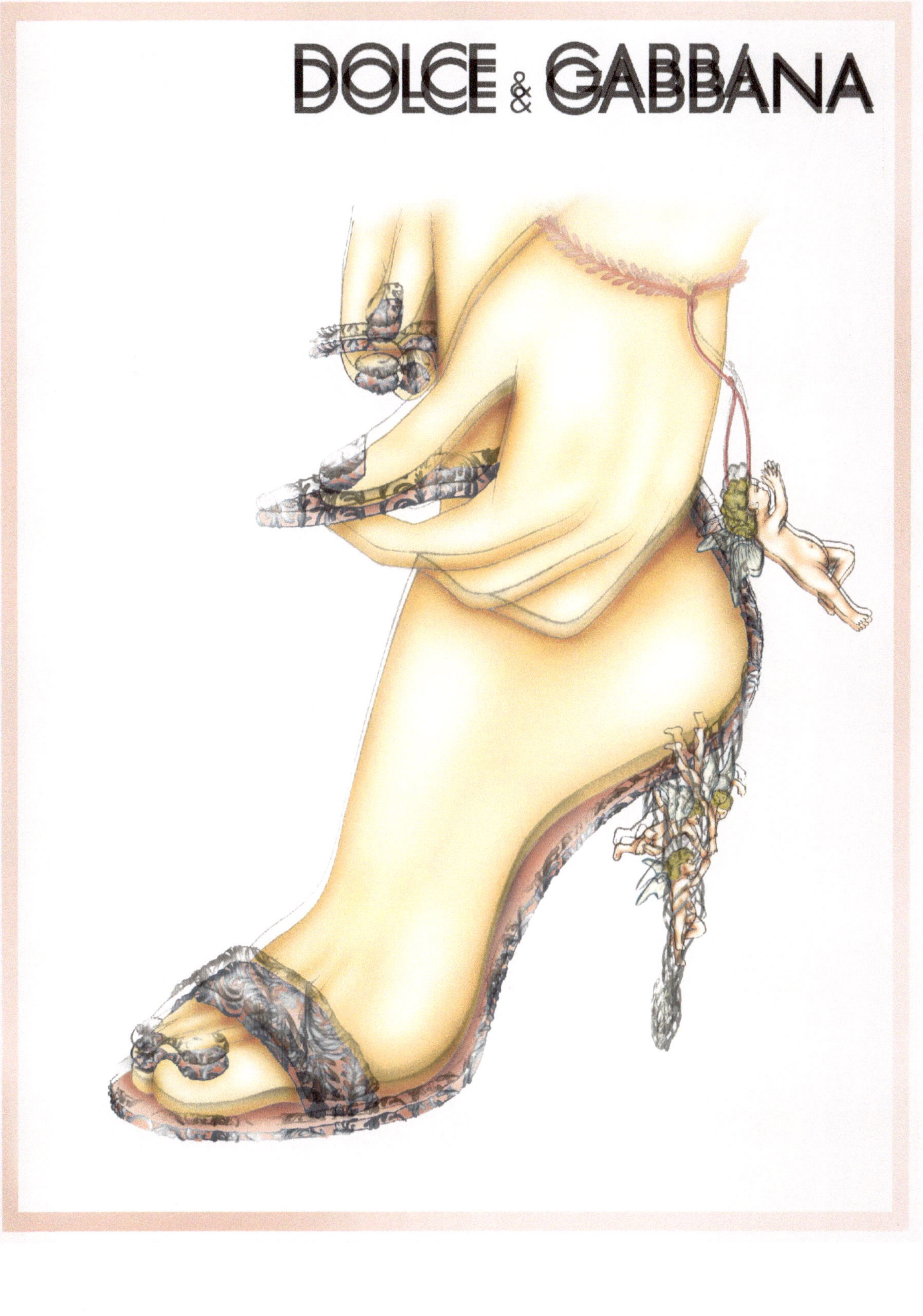

Milan Fashion Campus

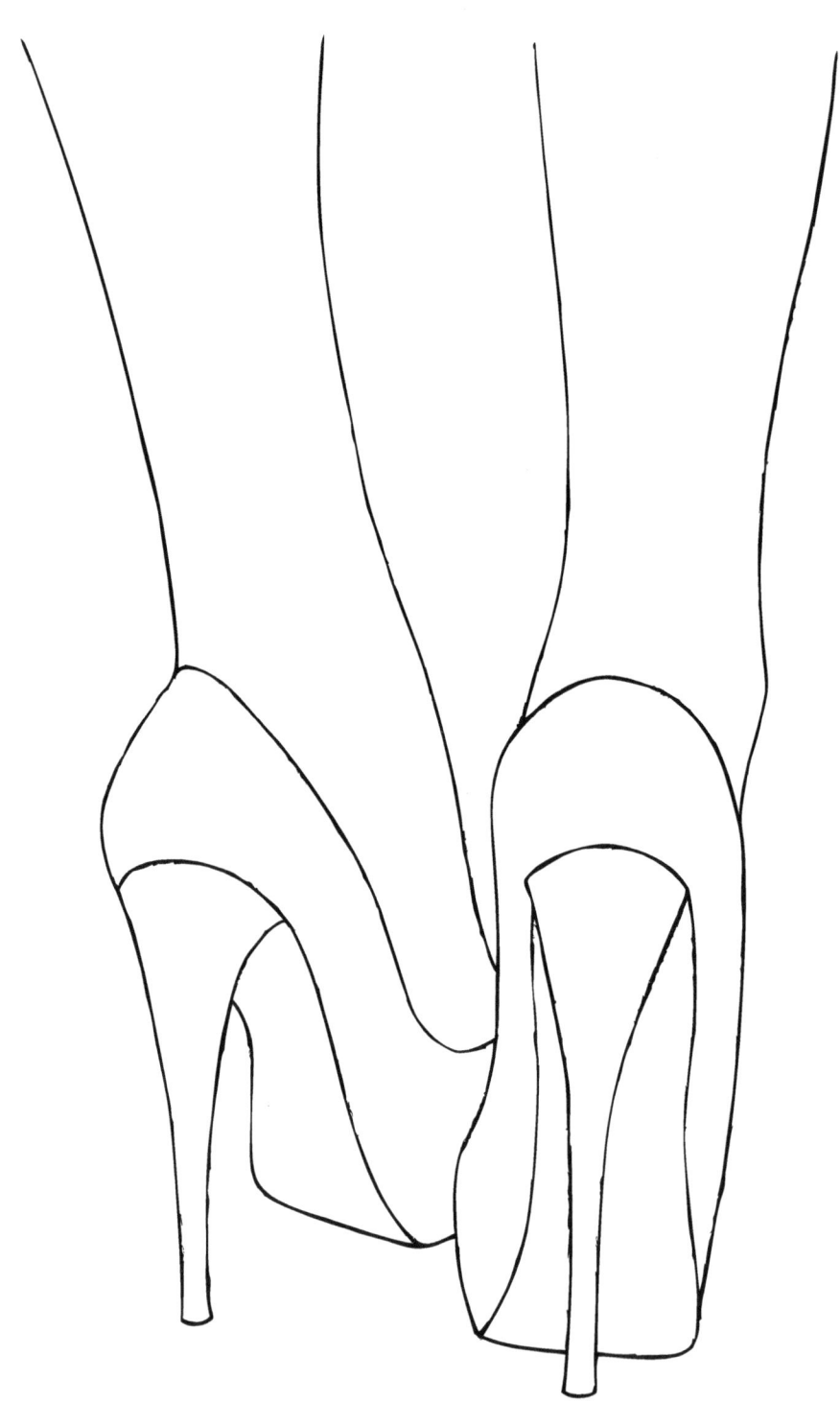

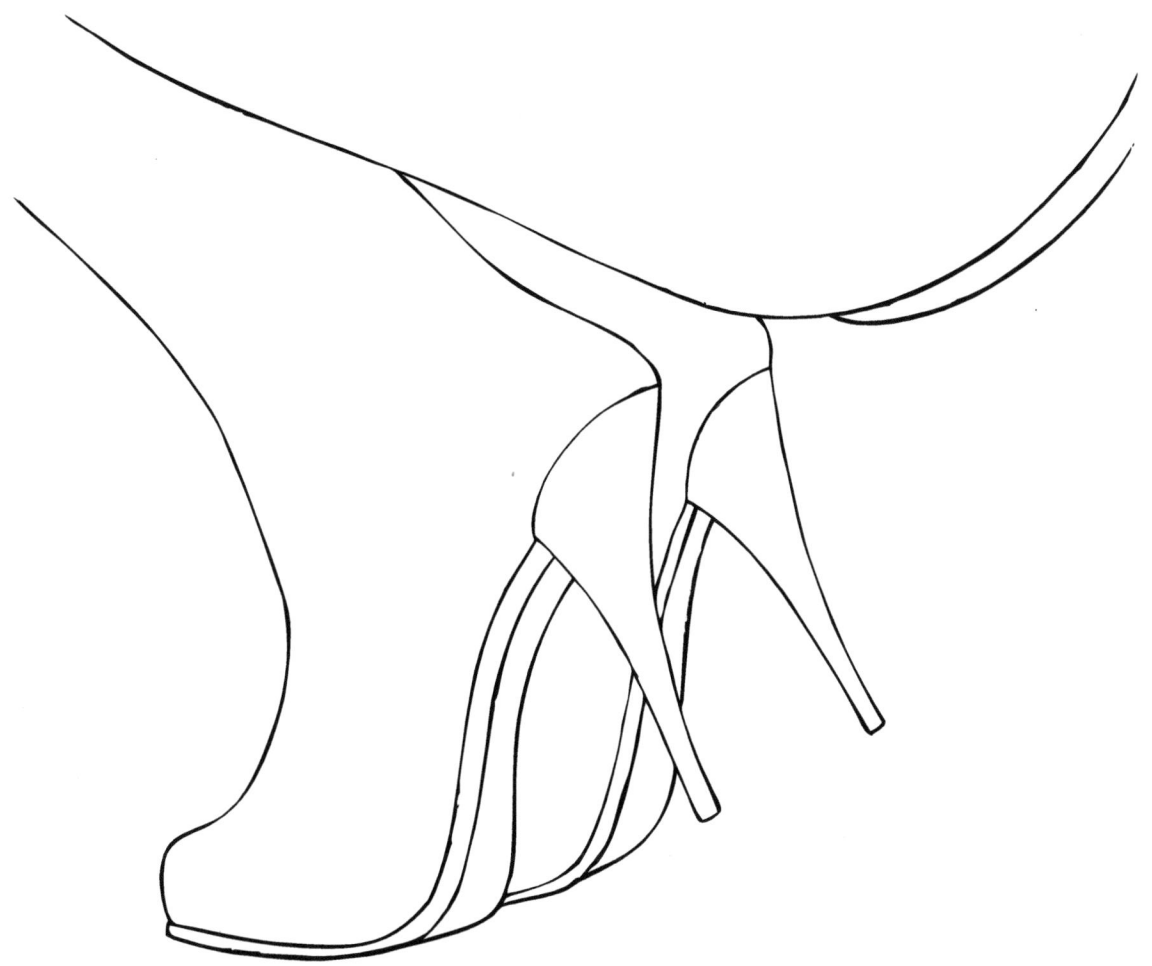

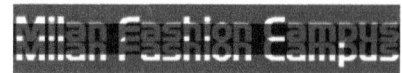

SENSUAL FASHION ILLUSTRATION

Milan Fashion Campus®
WWW.MILANFASHIONCAMPUS.EU